THE ORTHODOX LITURGY

The Greek Text with a completely new translation

followed by

- Notes on the text -

- The Sunday Gospel and Apostolic readings -

•

Foreword by

Archbishop Iakovos
Primate of the Greek Orthodox Church
in the Americas

•

by

Rev. Nicon D. Patrinacos
M.A., D. Phil. (Oxon.)

First published, February 1974.

Abridged edition, March 1974.

Published by:

THE GRAPHIC ARTS PRESS
611 SOUTH AVE.
GARWOOD, NEW JERSEY 07027

1974

TO

OUR AMERICAN ORTHODOX CONGREGATIONS

WHO

IN PRIDE AND HUMILITY

ABIDE BY THE FAITH OF THEIR FATHERS

ABOUT THIS ABRIDGED EDITION

This edition is an abridged form of the regular 352 page edition. The following have been left out: Communion Prayers (11 pages), and the entire Part II of the book dealing with the development of the Orthodox Liturgy from the 2nd century to this day (148 pages).

The Foreword by Archbishop Iakovos, together with the author's *About this Book,* have been retained in this abridged edition because they give a precise indication of the entire contents of the book and of its main theme and manner of treatment. Readers wishing a closer contact with our Liturgy, more lasting and more enlightening than the one afforded by reading the translation, are urged to consult the regular edition.

CONTENTS

This liturgical study, the outcome of extensive research and painstaking work, is the fruit of a broader spiritual endeavor in the field of Orthodox liturgics undertaken by the already well-known learned theologian, the Very Reverend Nicon D. Patrinacos.

It is recommended to you — the young and the old, the Orthodox and the non-Orthodox — as a truly new liturgical text, a guide and companion for worshipping in church or in private; no less, as a most informative, original in many respects, and personally useful, inspirational and edifying book.

Now that so many among us earnestly dwell on the subject of personal spiritual renewal, we should remind ourselves of our very limited knowledge of our Divine Liturgy and the most fundamental teachings of our Orthodox theology. Let us, then, try to rediscover both the genuine Orthodox doctrine and our precious liturgical practice and tradition.

Dr. Patrinacos' book introduces us to a deeper knowledge of our liturgical practice, and will certainly enrich the reader's appreciation of the depth, beauty, and spirituality of our Byzantine Liturgy and worship.

Archbishop Iakovos
Primate of the Greek Orthodox Church
in the Americas

Christmas, 1973

ABOUT THIS BOOK

The purpose and nature of this book are self-evident for anyone who would care to go through it even cursorily. The need for a book of this nature has, indeed, been a pressing one for the English speaking Orthodox who, apart from translations of the text of the Liturgy, knows practically nothing about the manner this text developed through the ages and the reasons for which it has finally taken its present form and contents.

By revealing for the first time — in terms of lay understanding — the historical, theological, and cultural influences that from the 2nd century to this day have worked together to make our Liturgy what it is, the true essence of it as well as its extraneous appendices come to light; the former to draw our attention to and increase our appreciation of this treasure of ours, the latter to afford us a healthy perspective of what is really genuine in it and what is not.

This uncovering could also serve as a thorough commentary on the contents of the Liturgy. As a result of their placement in historical and ecclesiastical perspective, their inherent devotional zest together with their spiritual value emerge fully and unmistakably for the individual believer as well as the group.

The notes on the Greek text are intended for those who would like to have textual and other reasons for our particular translation of certain terms and passages. But even those who know no Greek may find them helpful in other respects.

My debts to authors and writings are long-standing and too numerous to be acknowledged here by reference to names and works. However, my deepest appreciation goes to the Primate of the Greek Orthodox Church in the Americas, Archbishop Iakovos, not only for his generous Foreword, but for pointing out to me the need for a study in the nature of the second part of this book.

My dedicating this book to American Orthodox Congregations is intended to humbly point out our responsibilities toward our future above and beyond considerations other than our primary concern for our genuine Orthodox experience.

N. D. P.

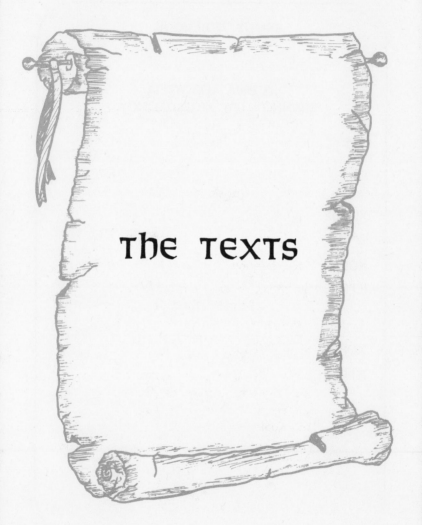

THE TEXTS

Η ΘΕΙΑ ΛΕΙΤΟΥΡΓΙΑ
ΙΩΑΝΝΟΥ ΤΟΥ ΧΡΥΣΟΣΤΟΜΟΥ

ΙΕΡΕΥΣ : Εὐλογημένη ἡ Βασιλεία
τοῦ Πατρός, καὶ τοῦ Υἱοῦ, καὶ τοῦ Ἁγίου
[Πνεύματος,
νῦν καὶ ἀεὶ καὶ εἰς τοὺς αἰῶνας τῶν αἰώνων.

ΧΟΡΟΣ : Ἀμήν.

ΙΕΡΕΥΣ : Ἐν εἰρήνῃ τοῦ Κυρίου δεηθῶμεν.

ΧΟΡΟΣ : Κύριε ἐλέησον.

ΙΕΡΕΥΣ : Ὑπὲρ τῆς ἄνωθεν εἰρήνης
καὶ τῆς σωτηρίας τῶν ψυχῶν ἡμῶν,
τοῦ Κυρίου δεηθῶμεν.

ΧΟΡΟΣ : Κύριε ἐλέησον.

ΙΕΡΕΥΣ : Ὑπὲρ τῆς εἰρήνης τοῦ σύμπαντος κόσμου,
εὐσταθείας τῶν ἁγίων τοῦ Θεοῦ Ἐκκλησιῶν
καὶ τῆς τῶν πάντων ἑνώσεως,
τοῦ Κυρίου δεηθῶμεν.

ΧΟΡΟΣ : Κύριε ἐλέησον.

THE DIVINE LITURGY
OF ST. JOHN CHRYSOSTOM

PRIEST : Blessed be the kingdom   (1)*
of the Father, and of the Son,
and of the Holy Spirit,
now, and ever, and for evermore.

PEOPLE: Amen.

PRIEST : In peace, let us pray to the Lord.   (2)

PEOPLE: Kyrie eleison (Lord, have mercy).

PRIEST : For the peace from God
and for the salvation of our souls,
let us pray to the Lord.

PEOPLE: Kyrie eleison (Lord, have mercy).

PRIEST : For the peace of the whole world,
for the well-being of the holy Churches

                        [of God
and for the union of all people,   (3)
let us pray to the Lord.

PEOPLE: Kyrie eleison (Lord, have mercy).

ΙΕΡΕΥΣ: Ὑπὲρ τοῦ ἁγίου Οἴκου τούτου,
καὶ τῶν μετὰ πίστεως,
εὐλαβείας καὶ φόβου Θεοῦ εἰσιόντων ἐν αὐτῷ,
τοῦ Κυρίου δεηθῶμεν.

ΧΟΡΟΣ: Κύριε ἐλέησον.

ΙΕΡΕΥΣ: Ὑπὲρ τοῦ Ἀρχιεπισκόπου ἡμῶν ....,
τοῦ τιμίου Πρεσβυτερίου, τῆς ἐν Χριστῷ
[διακονίας,
παντὸς τοῦ κλήρου καὶ τοῦ λαοῦ,
τοῦ Κυρίου δεηθῶμεν.

ΙΕΡΕΥΣ: Ὑπὲρ τοῦ θεοσεβοῦς Προέδρου ἡμῶν..........,
παντὸς τοῦ Ἀμερικανικοῦ λαοῦ καὶ τοῦ
[Ἑλληνικοῦ Ἔθνους,
τοῦ Κυρίου δεηθῶμεν.

ΧΟΡΟΣ: Κύριε ἐλέησον.

ΙΕΡΕΥΣ: Ὑπὲρ τῆς πόλεως ταύτης,
πάσης πόλεως, χώρας,
καὶ τῶν πίστει οἰκούντων ἐν αὐταῖς,
τοῦ Κυρίου δεηθῶμεν.

ΧΟΡΟΣ: Κύριε ἐλέησον.

ΙΕΡΕΥΣ: Ὑπὲρ εὐκρασίας ἀέρων,
εὐφορίας τῶν καρπῶν τῆς γῆς,
καὶ καιρῶν εἰρηνικῶν,
τοῦ Κυρίου δεηθῶμεν.

PRIEST : For this holy temple,
for those who enter it with faith,
reverence, and the fear of God,
let us in prayer ask of the Lord.

PEOPLE: Kyrie eleison (Lord, have mercy).

PRIEST : For our Archbishop . . . . .
the venerable presbyters, the deacons in the
service of Christ, and for all the clergy
and the laity,   (4)
let us in prayer ask of the Lord.

PEOPLE: Kyrie eleison (Lord, have mercy).
For our President,
and for those in civil authority and in the
service of the defense of our country,
let us in prayer ask of the Lord.

PEOPLE: Kyrie eleison (Lord, have mercy).

PRIEST : For this parish and this city,
for every city and every country,
and for those who live in the faith therein
let us in prayer ask of the Lord.

PEOPLE: Kyrie eleison (Lord, have mercy).

PRIEST : For mild weather,   (5)
for an abundance of the fruits of the earth,
and for temperate seasons,
let us in prayer ask of the Lord.

ΧΟΡΟΣ: Κύριε ἐλέησον.

ΙΕΡΕΥΣ: Ὑπὲρ πλεόντων, ὁδοιπορούντων,
νοσούντων, καμνόντων,
αἰχμαλώτων, καὶ τῆς σωτηρίας αὐτῶν,
τοῦ Κυρίου δεηθῶμεν.

ΧΟΡΟΣ: Κύριε ἐλέησον.

ΙΕΡΕΥΣ: Ὑπὲρ τοῦ ρυσθῆναι ἡμᾶς ἀπὸ πάσης θλίψεως,
ὀργῆς, κινδύνου καὶ ἀνάγκης,
τοῦ Κυρίου δεηθῶμεν.

ΧΟΡΟΣ: Κύριε ἐλέησον.

ΙΕΡΕΥΣ: Ἀντιλαβοῦ, σῶσον, ἐλέησον,
καὶ διαφύλαξον ἡμᾶς, ὁ Θεός,
τῇ Σῇ χάριτι.
Τῆς Παναγίας Ἀχράντου, ὑπερευλογημένης,
ἐνδόξου Δεσποίνης ἡμῶν Θεοτόκου
[καὶ ἀειπαρθένου Μαρίας,
μετὰ πάντων τῶν ἁγίων μνημονεύσαντες,
ἑαυτοὺς καὶ ἀλλήλους καὶ πᾶσαν τὴν ζωὴν
[ἡμῶν,
Χριστῷ τῷ Θεῷ παραθώμεθα.

ΧΟΡΟΣ: Σοί, Κύριε.

ΙΕΡΕΥΣ: (μυστικῶς)
Κύριε ὁ Θεὸς ἡμῶν, οὗ τὸ κράτος ἀνείκαστον
καὶ ἡ δόξα ἀκατάληπτος,
οὗ τὸ ἔλεος ἀμέτρητον καὶ ἡ φιλανθρωπία ἄφατος,
αὐτὸς Δέσποτα κατὰ τὴν σὴν εὐσπλαγχνίαν

PEOPLE: Kyrie eleison (Lord, have mercy).

PRIEST : For those at sea,
for those who travel by land or by air,
for the sick, the suffering, the captive,
and for their safety and salvation, (6)
let us in prayer ask of the Lord.

PEOPLE: Kyrie eleison (Lord, have mercy).

PRIEST : For our deliverance from affliction, (7)
wrath, danger, and want,
let us in prayer ask of the Lord.

PEOPLE: Kyrie eleison (Lord, have mercy).

PRIEST : Help us, save us, have mercy and keep us,(8)
our Lord, by Thy Grace.
Let us reverently bring to mind our most
holy, pure, blessed, and glorious Lady, (9)
Mother of God and ever-virgin Mary with
[all the saints,
and let us commit ourselves,
one another and our whole life
to Christ our God.

PEOPLE: To Thee, our Lord (Slowly). (10)

PRIEST : (inaudibly):
Lord, our God, whose power we cannot conceive
and the glory cannot comprehend;
whose mercy is boundless, and love for man
beyond words.

ἐπίβλεψον ἐφ᾽ ἡμᾶς καὶ ἐπὶ τὸν ἅγιον οἶκον τοῦτον
καὶ ποίησον μεθ᾽ ἡμῶν καὶ τῶν συνευχομένων ἡμῖν
πλούσια τὰ ἐλέη σου καὶ τοὺς οἰκτιρμούς σου.

ΙΕΡΕΥΣ : Ὅτι πρέπει σοι πᾶσα δόξα, τιμὴ καὶ
προσκύνησις,
τῷ Πατρί, καὶ τῷ Υἱῷ, καὶ τῷ Ἁγίῳ
[Πνεύματι,
νῦν καὶ ἀεί, καὶ εἰς τοὺς αἰῶνας τῶν αἰώνων.

ΧΟΡΟΣ : Ἀμήν.

ΑΝΤΙΦΩΝΟΝ Α´

ΧΟΡΟΣ : Ταῖς πρεσβείαις τῆς Θεοτόκου, Σῶτερ,
σῶσον ἡμᾶς. (τρὶς)

ΙΕΡΕΥΣ : Ἔτι καὶ ἔτι, ἐν εἰρήνη τοῦ Κυρίου δεηθῶμεν.

ΧΟΡΟΣ : Κύριε ἐλέησον.

ΙΕΡΕΥΣ : Ἀντιλαβοῦ, σῶσον, ἐλέησον
καὶ διαφύλαξον ἡμᾶς, ὁ Θεός,
τῇ σῇ χάριτι.

ΧΟΡΟΣ : Κύριε ἐλέησον.

ΙΕΡΕΥΣ : Τῆς Παναγίας Ἀχράντου, ὑπερευλογημένης,
ἐνδόξου Δεσποίνης ἡμῶν Θεοτόκου,
[καὶ Ἀειπαρθένου Μαρίας
μετὰ πάντων τῶν ἁγίων μνημονεύσαντες,

Look down upon us in Thy compassion, Master,
and upon this holy House,
and make that Thy mercy and compassion be
[richly bestowed
upon us and upon those who pray with us;
(audibly)
. . . for, to Thee belong glory, honor, and
[worship,
to the Father, and to the Son, and to the
[Holy Spirit,
now, and ever, and for evermore.

PEOPLE: Amen.

The First Antiphon

PEOPLE: By the intercessions of the Mother of God
Savior, save us. (Three times)

PRIEST : Let us again in peace implore the Lord.

PEOPLE: Kyrie eleison (Lord, have mercy).

PRIEST : Help us, save us, have mercy on us,
and keep us, our God, by Thy Grace.

PEOPLE: Kyrie eleison (Lord, have mercy).

PRIEST : Let us reverently bring to mind our most
[holy,
pure, blessed, and glorious Lady,
Mother of God and ever-virgin Mary with
[all the saints,

έαυτοὺς καὶ ἀλλήλους, καὶ πᾶσαν τὴν ζωὴν
[ἡμῶν,
Χριστῷ τῷ Θεῷ παραθώμεθα.

ΧΟΡΟΣ: Σοὶ Κύριε.

ΙΕΡΕΥΣ: (μυστικῶς)

Δέσποτα Κύριε, ὁ Θεὸς ἡμῶν, σῶσον τὸν λαόν σου καὶ
εὐλόγησον τὴν κληρονομίαν σου,
τὸ πλήρωμα τῆς Ἐκκλησίας σου φύλαξον,
ἁγίασον τοὺς ἀγαπῶντας τὴν εὐπρέπειαν τοῦ οἴκου σου.
Σὺ αὐτοὺς ἀντιδόξασον τῇ θεϊκῇ σου δυνάμει
καὶ μὴ ἐγκαταλείπης ἡμᾶς τοὺς ἐλπίζοντας ἐπὶ σέ.

ΙΕΡΕΥΣ: Ὅτι σὸν τὸ Κράτος καὶ Σοῦ ἐστιν ἡ Βασιλεία,
καὶ ἡ δύναμις, καὶ ἡ δόξα
τοῦ Πατρός, καὶ τοῦ Υἱοῦ, καὶ τοῦ Ἁγίου
[Πνεύματος,
νῦν καὶ ἀεί, καὶ εἰς τοὺς αἰῶνας τῶν αἰώνων.

ΧΟΡΟΣ: Ἀμήν.

ΑΝΤΙΦΩΝΟΝ Β΄

ΧΟΡΟΣ: Σῶσον ἡμᾶς, Υἱὲ Θεοῦ, ὁ ἀναστὰς ἐκ
[νεκρῶν,
ψάλλοντάς Σοι Ἀλληλούϊα. (δὶς)
Δόξα Πατρὶ καὶ Υἱῷ καὶ ἁγίῳ Πνεύματι.
Καὶ νῦν, καὶ ἀεί, καὶ εἰς τοὺς αἰῶνας τῶν
[αἰώνων, Ἀμήν.
Ὁ μονογενὴς Υἱὸς καὶ Λόγος τοῦ Θεοῦ

and let us commit ourselves,
one another and our whole life
to Christ our God.

PEOPLE: To Thee, our Lord.

PRIEST : (inaudibly)
Master, Lord our God,
save Thy people and bless Thy inheritors;
protect all the members of Thy Church; (11)
sanctify those who love the beauty of
Thy house; glorify them in return by Thy divine
[power;
and do not forsake us who place our hope in Thee.

PRIEST : (audibly)
for Thine is the dominion, the kingdom, the
[power,
and the glory, of the Father, and of the Son,
and of the Holy Spirit,
now, and ever, and for evermore.

PEOPLE: Amen.

The Second Antiphon

PEOPLE: Son of God, who did rise from the dead,
save us who sing to Thee,
Alleluia! (Twice)
Glory to the Father and to the Son and to
[the Holy Spirit,
now, and ever, and for evermore.
Only-begotten Son and Word of God, (12)

ἀθάνατος ὑπάρχων,
καὶ καταδεξάμενος, διὰ τὴν ἡμετέραν
                                    [σωτηρίαν,
σαρκωθῆναι ἐκ τῆς ἁγίας Θεοτόκου καὶ
ἀειπαρθένου Μαρίας,
ἀτρέπτως ἐνανθρωπήσας·
σταυρωθείς τε Χριστὲ ὁ Θεός,
θανάτῳ θάνατον πατήσας,
εἷς ὢν τῆς ἁγίας Τριάδος
συνδοξαζόμενος τῷ Πατρὶ καὶ τῷ ἁγίῳ
                                    [Πνεύματι,
σῶσον ἡμᾶς.

ΙΕΡΕΥΣ : Ἔτι καὶ ἔτι ἐν εἰρήνῃ τοῦ Κυρίου δεηθῶμεν.

ΧΟΡΟΣ : Κύριε ἐλέησον.

ΙΕΡΕΥΣ : Ἀντιλαβοῦ, σῶσον, ἐλέησον
καὶ διαφύλαξον ἡμᾶς,
ὁ Θεός, τῇ Σῇ χάριτι.

ΧΟΡΟΣ : Κύριε ἐλέησον.

ΙΕΡΕΥΣ : Τῆς Παναγίας, ἀχράντου, ὑπερευλογημένης,
ἐνδόξου Δεσποίνης ἡμῶν Θεοτόκου
                    [καὶ ἀειπαρθένου Μαρίας
μετὰ πάντων τῶν Ἁγίων μνημονεύσαντες
ἑαυτοὺς καὶ ἀλλήλους καὶ πᾶσαν τὴν ζωὴν
                                    [ἡμῶν,
Χριστῷ τῷ Θεῷ παραθώμεθα.

ΧΟΡΟΣ : Σοί, Κύριε.

being Immortal,
Thou humbled Thyself for our salvation,
taking flesh by the holy Mother of God and
                              [ever-virgin Mary;
Thou became man without change,
and were crucified,
thereby destroying death by death;   (13)
being one of the Holy Trinity,
together glorified with the Father and
the Holy Spirit;
Save us, Christ our God!

PRIEST : Let us again in peace implore the Lord.

PEOPLE: Kyrie eleison (Lord, have mercy).

PRIEST : Help us, save us, have mercy on us,
and keep us our God,
by Thy Grace.

PEOPLE: Kyrie eleison (Lord, have mercy).

PRIEST : Let us respectfully call to mind our most
                                  [holy,
pure, blessed, and glorious Lady,
Mother of God and ever-virgin Mary,
with all the saints,
and let us commit ourselves,
one another and our whole life
to Christ our God.

PEOPLE: To Thee, our God. (Slowly)

ΙΕΡΕΥΣ : (μυστικῶς)

Ὁ τὰς κοινὰς ταύτας
καὶ συμφώνους ἡμῖν χαρισάμενος προσευχάς,
ὁ καὶ δυσὶ καὶ τρισὶ συμφωνοῦσιν ἐπὶ τῷ ὀνόματί σου
τὰς αἰτήσεις παρέχειν ἐπαγγειλάμενος
αὐτὸς καὶ νῦν τῶν δούλων σου τὰ αἰτήματα πρὸς τὸ συμφέρον
[πλήρωσον,
χορηγῶν ἡμῖν ἐν τῷ παρόντι αἰῶνι τὴν ἐπίγνωσιν τῆς σῆς
[ἀληθείας
καὶ ἐν τῷ μέλλοντι ζωὴν αἰώνιον χαριζόμενος.

ΙΕΡΕΥΣ : Ὅτι ἀγαθὸς καὶ φιλάνθρωπος Θεὸς ὑπάρχεις
καὶ σοὶ τὴν δόξαν ἀναπέμπομεν,
τῷ Πατρί, καὶ τῷ Υἱῷ, καὶ τῷ Ἁγίῳ Πνεύματι,
νῦν καὶ ἀεὶ καὶ εἰς τοὺς αἰῶνας τῶν αἰώνων.

ΧΟΡΟΣ : Ἀμήν.

ΙΕΡΕΥΣ : (μυστικῶς)

Δέσποτα Κύριε, ὁ Θεὸς ἡμῶν,
ὁ καταστήσας ἐν οὐρανοῖς
τάγματα καὶ στρατιὰς ἀγγέλων καὶ ἀρχαγγέλων,
εἰς λειτουργίαν τῆς σῆς δόξης,
ποίησον σὺν τῇ εἰσόδῳ ἡμῶν εἴσοδον ἁγίων ἀγγέλων γενέσθαι,
συλλειτουργούντων ἡμῖν καὶ συνδοξολογούντων τὴν σὴν
[ἀγαθότητα.
Ὅτι πρέπει σοι πᾶσα δόξα, τιμὴ καὶ προσκύνησις,
τῷ Πατρί, καὶ τῷ Υἱῷ, καὶ τῷ Ἁγίῳ Πνεύματι,
νῦν καὶ ἀεὶ καὶ εἰς τοὺς αἰῶνας τῶν αἰώνων.

PRIEST : (inaudibly)
Thou who have allowed us to offer
these common supplications with one heart,
who have promised to grant the requests of two
or three gathered in Thy name,
satisfy now the petitions of Thy servants
to our best interest,
granting us the knowledge of Thy truth in this life
and life everlasting in the age to come;
(audibly)

for, Thou are a Good and loving God,
and to Thee we ascribe glory,
to the Father and to the Son, and to the
[Holy Spirit,
now, and ever, and for evermore.

PEOPLE: Amen. (The hymn of the day, Apolytikion,
[is sung). (14)

PRIEST : (inaudibly)
Master and Lord, our God, who have instituted in
heaven the orders and hosts of Angels and
[Archangels
to minister to Thy glory,
grant that we may be accompanied into Thy
[sanctuary
by the holy Angels and together minister and
glorify Thy goodness.
For, to Thee belong glory, honor, and worship,
to the Father, and to the Son, and to the Holy
[Spirit,
now, and ever, and for evermore. Amen.

ΕΙΣΟΔΟΣ ΤΟΥ ΕΥΑΓΓΕΛΙΟΥ

(Τὸ σημεῖον τοῦτο τῆς Θείας Λειτουργίας
συμβολίζει τὴν ἔλευσιν τοῦ Χριστοῦ, ὁ ὁποῖος
εἶναι ἡ Σοφία τοῦ Θεοῦ, εἰς τὴν γῆν.
Ὁ Χορὸς ψάλλει ἓν τῶν Ἀναστασίμων
Ἀπολυτικίων. Ὁ Ἱερεὺς ἐξέρχεται ἀπὸ τὸ
Ἅγιον Βῆμα κρατῶν τὸ Εὐαγγέλιον.
Ἐμπρὸς πηγαίνουν τὰ παιδιὰ τοῦ Ἱεροῦ
μὲ λαμπάδες. Πρὸ τῆς Ἁγίας Πύλης τοῦ
Εἰκονοστασίου, ὑψώνει τὸ Εὐαγγέλιον καὶ λέγει):

ΙΕΡΕΥΣ : Σοφία, ὀρθοί.

ΧΟΡΟΣ : Δεῦτε προσκυνήσωμεν καὶ προσπέσωμεν
[Χριστῷ.
Σῶσον ἡμᾶς, Υἱὲ Θεοῦ,
ὁ ἀναστὰς ἐκ νεκρῶν,
ψάλλοντάς Σοι Ἀλληλούϊα.

ΙΕΡΕΥΣ : Τοῦ Κυρίου δεηθῶμεν.

ΧΟΡΟΣ : Κύριε ἐλέησον.

ΙΕΡΕΥΣ : Ὅτι ἅγιος εἶ ὁ Θεὸς ἡμῶν,
καὶ σοὶ τὴν δόξαν ἀναπέμπομεν,
τῷ Πατρὶ καὶ τῷ Υἱῷ καὶ τῷ ἁγίῳ Πνεύματι,
νῦν καὶ ἀεὶ καὶ εἰς τοὺς αἰῶνας τῶν αἰώνων.

ΧΟΡΟΣ : Ἀμήν.
Ἅγιος ὁ Θεός,
Ἅγιος Ἰσχυρός,
Ἅγιος Ἀθάνατος,
ἐλέησον ἡμᾶς. (τρὶς)

The Gospel Procession
(The Little Entrance) (15)

(The priest comes in procession before the Royal Gate raises the Gospel and proclaims:)

PRIEST : Wisdom! Let us stand!

PEOPLE: Come! Let us worship and bow down before
[Christ.
Son of God who did rise from the dead,
save us who sing to Thee.
Alleluia!
(The priest enters the sanctuary and hymns relating to the feast of the day are sung).

PRIEST : Let us pray to the Lord.

PEOPLE: Kyrie eleison (Lord, have mercy).

PRIEST : For, Thou are Holy, our God,
and to Thee we ascribe glory,
to the Father, and to the Son,
and to the Holy Spirit,
now, and ever, and for evermore.

PEOPLE: Amen

The Trisagion Hymn

PEOPLE: Holy God,
Holy and Mighty,
Holy and Immortal One,
have mercy on us. (Three times)

Δόξα Πατρὶ καὶ Υἱῷ καὶ ἁγίῳ Πνεύματι.
Καὶ νῦν καὶ ἀεὶ καὶ εἰς τοὺς αἰῶνας τῶν αἰώνων.
Ἀμήν.
Ἅγιος Ἀθάνατος, ἐλέησον ἡμᾶς.
Δύναμις. Ἅγιος ὁ Θεός,
Ἅγιος Ἰσχυρός,
Ἅγιος Ἀθάνατος,
ἐλέησον ἡμᾶς.

ΙΕΡΕΥΣ : (μυστικῶς)

Ὁ θεὸς ὁ ἅγιος, ὁ ἐν Ἁγίοις ἀναπαυόμενος,
ὁ Τρισαγίῳ φωνῇ ὑπὸ τῶν Σεραφεὶμ ἀνυμνούμενος καὶ ὑπὸ τῶν
[Χερουβὶμ δοξολογούμενος
καὶ ὑπὸ πάσης ἐπουρανίου δυνάμεως προσκυνούμενος·
ὁ ἐκ τοῦ μὴ ὄντος εἰς τὸ εἶναι παραγαγὼν τὰ σύμπαντα·
ὁ κτίσας τὸν ἄνθρωπον κατ' εἰκόνα σὴν καὶ ὁμοίωσιν,
καὶ παντί σου χαρίσματι κατακοσμήσας·
ὁ διδοὺς αἰτοῦντι σοφίαν καὶ σύνεσιν,
καὶ μὴ παρορῶν ἁμαρτάνοντα, ἀλλὰ θέμενος ἐπὶ σωτηρίᾳ
[μετάνοιαν·
ὁ καταξιώσας ἡμᾶς τοὺς ταπεινοὺς καὶ ἀναξίους δούλους σου
καὶ ἐν τῇ ὥρᾳ ταύτῃ στῆναι κατενώπιον τῆς δόξης τοῦ ἁγίου
[σου θυσιαστηρίου
καὶ τὴν ὀφειλομένην σοι προσκύνησιν καὶ δοξολογίαν προσάγειν·
Αὐτός, Δέσποτα,
πρόσδεξαι καὶ ἐκ στόματος ἡμῶν τῶν ἁμαρτωλῶν τὸν τρι-
[σάγιον ὕμνον
καὶ ἐπίσκεψαι ἡμᾶς ἐν τῇ χρηστότητί σου·

24

Glory to the Father, and to the Son,
and to the Holy Spirit;
now, and ever, and for evermore. Amen.
. . . . Holy Immortal One, have mercy on us.
(Forte) Holy God,
Holy and Mighty,
Holy and Immortal One,
have mercy on us.
(While the above Trisagion hymn is sung,
the priest prays as follows:)

PRIEST : (inaudibly)

Holy God, who dwell in Thy saints   (16)
and are praised by the Seraphim with the thrice-
                                        [holy hymn,
who are glorified by the Cherubim and worshipped
by all the powers of heaven;
Thou who have brought all things to being from
                                        [non-being,
who have created man in Thy image and likeness
and have adorned him with all the gifts of
                                        [Thy Grace;
Thou who give wisdom and prudence to those
who would petition for them,
and do not overlook the sinner but have decreed
the way of repentance for his salvation;
Thou who have made us worthy to stand at this
                                        [time
before the glory of Thy holy altar,
humble and unworthy as we are,
and to offer the glory and worship that are owed
                                        [Thee;
Thou, Master, accept the thrice-holy hymn
even from the mouths of us the sinners
and visit us in Thy goodness;

συγχώρησον ἡμῖν πᾶν πλημμέλημα ἑκούσιόν τε καὶ ἀκούσιον,
ἁγίασον ἡμῶν τὰς ψυχὰς καὶ τὰ σώματα,
καὶ δὸς ἡμῖν ἐν ὁσιότητι λατρεύειν σοι πάσας τὰς ἡμέρας τῆς
[ζωῆς ἡμῶν·
πρεσβείαις τῆς ἁγίας Θεοτόκου καὶ πάντων τῶν ἁγίων
τῶν ἀπ᾽ αἰῶνός σοι εὐαρεστησάντων·
ὅτι ἅγιος εἶ ὁ Θεὸς ἡμῶν
καὶ σοὶ τὴν δόξαν ἀναπέμπομεν
τῷ Πατρί, καὶ τῷ Υἱῷ, καὶ τῷ Ἁγίῳ Πνεύματι,
νῦν, καὶ ἀεί, καὶ εἰς τοὺς αἰῶνας τῶν αἰώνων. Ἀμήν.

ΑΠΟΣΤΟΛΟΣ

ΙΕΡΕΥΣ : Πρόσχωμεν. Σοφία. Πρόσχωμεν.

ΑΝΑΓΝ : (Ἀναγινώσκει ἐκ τῆς ὡρισμένης περικοπῆς)

ΙΕΡΕΥΣ : (μυστικῶς)

Ἔλλαμψον ἐν ταῖς καρδίαις ἡμῶν,
φιλάνθρωπε Δέσποτα,
τὸ τῆς σῆς θεογνωσίας ἀκήρατον φῶς,
καὶ τοὺς τῆς διανοίας ἡμῶν διάνοιξον ὀφθαλμοὺς
εἰς τὴν τῶν εὐαγγελικῶν σου κηρυγμάτων κατανόησιν.
Ἔνθες ἡμῖν καὶ τὸν τῶν μακαρίων σου ἐντολῶν φόβον,
ἵνα τὰς σαρκικὰς ἐπιθυμίας καταπατήσαντες,

forgive our transgressions,
intentional and unintentional;
sanctify our souls and bodies
and grant that we may serve Thee in holiness
for the rest of our lives;
by the intercessions of the Holy Mother of God
and of all the saints who have pleased Thee
even from the beginning of time.
For, Thou are Holy, our God, and to Thee
we ascribe glory, to the Father, and
to the Son, and to the Holy Spirit,
now, and ever, and for evermore. Amen.

The Epistle

PRIEST : Let us attend!

READER: (Reads the introductory verses to the
Apostolic passage of the day).

PRIEST : Wisdom!

READER: The lesson is from . . . (the book of the
New Testament is given from which
he is to read).

PRIEST : Let us attend!

READER: (Reads the Apostolic Lesson).

PRIEST : (While the Apostolic reading is in process,
the priest prays inaudibly).

Illumine our hearts, merciful Master,
with the pure and unfading light of our knowl-
[edge of Thee,
and open the eyes of our mind to
comprehend fully the message of Thy Gospel.
And instill in us feared respect for Thy blessed
commandments, that, having conquered the
[desires

πνευματικὴν πολιτείαν μετέλθωμεν
πάντα τὰ πρὸς εὐαρέστησιν τὴν σὴν καὶ φρονοῦντες καὶ
[πράττοντες.
Σὺ γὰρ εἶ ὁ φωτισμὸς τῶν ψυχῶν καὶ τῶν σωμάτων ἡμῶν,
Χριστὲ ὁ Θεός,
καὶ σοὶ τὴν δόξαν ἀναπέμπομεν
σὺν τῷ ἀνάρχῳ σου Πατρί, καὶ τῷ παναγίῳ, καὶ ἀγαθῷ,
καὶ ζωοποιῷ σου Πνεύματι,
νῦν καὶ ἀεὶ καὶ εἰς τοὺς αἰῶνας τῶν αἰώνων. Ἀμήν.

ΙΕΡΕΥΣ : Εἰρήνη σοι τῷ ἀναγινώσκοντι.

ΧΟΡΟΣ : Ἀλληλούϊα. (τρὶς)

ΤΟ ΕΥΑΓΓΕΛΙΟΝ

ΙΕΡΕΥΣ : Σοφία, ὀρθοί.
Ἀκούσωμεν τοῦ Ἁγίου Εὐαγγελίου.
Εἰρήνη πᾶσι.

ΧΟΡΟΣ : Καὶ τῷ πνεύματί σου.

ΙΕΡΕΥΣ : Ἐκ τοῦ κατὰ (ὄνομα Εὐαγγελιστοῦ)
ἁγίου εὐαγγελίου τὸ ἀνάγνωσμα.
Πρόσχωμεν.

ΧΟΡΟΣ : Δόξα σοι, Κύριε, δόξα σοι.

ΙΕΡΕΥΣ : (Ἀναγινώσκει ἐκ τῆς ὡρισμένης περικοπῆς)

ΧΟΡΟΣ : Δόξα σοι, Κύριε, δόξα σοι.

ΙΕΡΕΥΣ : (μυστικῶς)

Πάλιν καὶ πολλάκις σοί προσπίπτομεν,
καὶ σοῦ δεόμεθα, ἀγαθὲ καὶ φιλάνθρωπε,
ὅπως ἐπιβλέψας ἐπὶ τὴν δέησιν ἡμῶν,
καθαρίσῃς ἡμῶν τὰς ψυχὰς καὶ τὰ σώματα
ἀπὸ παντὸς μολυσμοῦ σαρκὸς καὶ πνεύματος

of the flesh, we may take part in the life
of the Spirit, and do all the things
that are pleasing to Thee.
For, Thou, Christ our Lord, are
the light of our souls and bodies
and to Thee we ascribe glory,
together with Thy Father who is without
[beginning,
and Thy all-holy, good, and life-giving Spirit,
now and ever, and for evermore. Amen.

PRIEST : (To the Reader at the end of his reading:)
Peace be with you.

PEOPLE: Alleluia, Alleluia, Alleluia.

PRIEST : Wisdom! Arise! Let us listen to the Holy
[Gospel.
Peace be to all.

PEOPLE: And to your spirit.

The Gospel Reading

PRIEST : The reading is from the Holy Gospel
[according to . . . . .
Let us attend!

PEOPLE: Glory to Thee, our Lord, glory to Thee!

PEOPLE: (At the end of the Gospel reading:)
Glory to Thee, our Lord, glory to Thee!
[(slowly)

PRIEST : (inaudibly)   (17)

Again and oftentimes we bow in prayer and we
[beseech Thee,
Good and Merciful One,
to consider favorably our supplications
and cleanse our souls and bodies
from all defilement of flesh and spirit;

καὶ δώῃς ἡμῖν ἀνένοχον καὶ ἀκατάκριτον τὴν παράστασιν τοῦ
[ἁγίου σου θυσιαστηρίου.
Χάρισαι δέ, ὁ Θεός, καὶ τοῖς συνευχομένοις ἡμῖν
προκοπὴν βίου καὶ πίστεως καὶ συνέσεως πνευματικῆς·
δὸς αὐτοῖς πάντοτε μετὰ φόβου καὶ ἀγάπης
λατρεύειν σοι ἀνενόχως
καὶ ἀκατακρίτως μετέχειν τῶν ἁγίων σου Μυστηρίων,
καὶ τῆς ἐπουρανίου σου βασιλείας ἀξιωθῆναι.
Ἀντιλαβοῦ, σῶσον, ἐλέησον,
καὶ διαφύλαξον ἡμᾶς,
ὁ Θεός, τῇ σῇ χάριτι·

ΙΕΡΕΥΣ : Ὅπως ὑπὸ τοῦ Κράτους σου πάντοτε φυ-
[λαττόμενοι,
σοὶ δόξαν ἀναπέμπομεν
τῷ Πατρί, καὶ τῷ Υἱῷ, καὶ τῷ Ἁγίῳ Πνεύματι,
νῦν καὶ ἀεὶ καὶ εἰς τοὺς αἰῶνας τῶν αἰώνων.

ΧΟΡΟΣ : Ἀμήν.

Οἱ τὰ Χερουβὶμ μυστικῶς εἰκονίζοντες,
καὶ τῇ ζωοποιῷ Τριάδι τὸν τρισάγιον ὕμνον
[προσάδοντες,
πᾶσαν τὴν βιωτικὴν ἀποθώμεθα μέριμναν,
ὡς τὸν Βασιλέα τῶν ὅλων ὑποδεξόμενοι.....

ΙΕΡΕΥΣ : (μυστικῶς)

Οὐδεὶς ἄξιος τῶν συνδεδεμένων
ταῖς σαρκικαῖς ἐπιθυμίαις καὶ ἡδοναῖς
προσέρχεσθαι ἢ προσεγγίζειν ἢ λειτουργεῖν σοι,

and to allow us to stand before Thy holy altar
without guilt or condemnation.
Also grant, our God, to those who pray with us
advancement in life, in faith, and in spiritual
understanding;
allow them to ever worship Thee
with fear and love,
to partake of Thy Holy Mysteries without guilt or
condemnation,
and to become worthy of Thy heavenly kingdom.
Help us, save us, have mercy on us, and keep us,
our God, by Thy Grace. Wisdom!

PRIEST : (audibly)
that ever being protected by Thy power,
to Thee we ascribe the glory,
to the Father, and to the Son, and to the
[Holy Spirit,
now and ever, and for evermore.

PEOPLE: Amen. (The hymn of the Cherubin follows:)
We, who mystically represent the Cherubim
and sing the thrice-holy hymn to the
life-giving Trinity,   (18)
let us lay aside the cares of life,
that we may receive the King of all . . . . .
(the hymn is interrupted at this point)

PRIEST : (While the Cherubic hymn is being sung,
the priest prays inaudibly:)
No one who is bound to the desires and pleasures
of the flesh is worthy of approaching, drawing
[near,

Βασιλεῦ τῆς δόξης· τὸ γὰρ διακονεῖν σοι μέγα
καὶ φοβερὸν καὶ αὐταῖς ταῖς ἐπουρανίαις
δυνάμεσιν. Ἀλλ᾽ ὅμως διὰ τὴν ἄφατον
καὶ ἀμέτρητόν σου φιλανθρωπίαν
ἀτρέπτως καὶ ἀναλλοιώτως γέγονας
ἄνθρωπος καὶ Ἀρχιερεὺς ἡμῶν ἐχρημάτισας,
καὶ τῆς λειτουργικῆς ταύτης καὶ ἀναιμάκτου θυσίας τὴν
ἱερουργίαν παρέδωκας ἡμῖν
ὡς Δεσπότης τῶν ἁπάντων.
Σὺ γὰρ μόνος, Κύριε ὁ Θεὸς ἡμῶν,
δεσπόζεις τῶν ἐπουρανίων καὶ τῶν ἐπιγείων,
ὁ ἐπὶ θρόνου χερουβικοῦ ἐποχούμενος,
ὁ τῶν Σεραφὶμ Κύριος καὶ Βασιλεὺς τοῦ Ἰσραήλ,
ὁ μόνος Ἅγιος καὶ ἐν Ἁγίοις ἀναπαυόμενος.
Σὲ τοίνυν δυσωπῶ τὸν μόνον ἀγαθὸν καὶ εὐήκοον.
Ἐπίβλεψον ἐπ᾽ ἐμὲ τὸν ἁμαρτωλὸν καὶ ἀχρεῖον δοῦλόν σου,
καὶ καθάρισόν μου τὴν ψυχὴν καὶ τὴν καρδίαν ἀπὸ
                              [συνειδήσεως πονηρᾶς
καὶ ἱκάνωσόν με τῇ δυνάμει τοῦ Ἁγίου σου Πνεύματος,
ἐνδεδυμένον τὴν τῆς ἱερατείας χάριν,
παραστῆναι τῇ ἁγίᾳ σου ταύτῃ Τραπέζῃ,
καὶ ἱερουργῆσαι τὸ ἅγιον καὶ ἄχραντόν σου Σῶμα καὶ τὸ
                              [τίμιον Αἷμα.
Σοὶ γὰρ προσέρχομαι,
κλίνας τὸν ἐμαυτοῦ αὐχένα, καὶ δέομαί σου.
Μὴ ἀποστρέψῃς τὸ πρόσωπόν σου ἀπ᾽ ἐμοῦ,
μηδὲ ἀποδοκιμάσῃς με ἐκ παίδων σου·
ἀλλ᾽ ἀξίωσον προσενεχθῆναί σοι
ὑπ᾽ ἐμοῦ τοῦ ἁμαρτωλοῦ δούλου σου τὰ Δῶρα ταῦτα.
Σὺ γὰρ εἶ ὁ προσφέρων καὶ προσφερόμενος

or ministering to Thee, King of glory;
for, to serve Thee is great and awesome
even to the heavenly Powers.
Yet, because of Thy love for us
which is beyond words and beyond measure,
Thou became man without change or differen-
[tiation,
served as our High Priest and entrusted to us,
as Lord of all,
the celebration of this liturgical and bloodless
[sacrifice.

For, Thou alone, Lord our God,
rule over all things in heaven and on earth;
who are borne on the Cherubic throne,
the Lord of the Seraphim and the King of Israel,
the only Holy One who dwell in Your Saints.
Therefore, I implore Thee
who alone are Good and ready to hear me:
look down upon me, Thy sinful and worthless
[servant,
and cleanse my soul and my heart from wicked
[conscience;
and make me able, by the power of Thy Holy
[Spirit,
vested with the Grace of priesthood,
to stand before this Thy holy altar
and consecrate Thy Holy and most pure Body
and Thy precious Blood.
To Thee I come with bowed head and I beg:
do not turn Thy face away from me,
nor sever me from among Thy children;
but make me worthy,
Thy sinner and unworthy servant,
to offer Thee these gifts.
For, Thou are the One
who do offer and are offered,

καὶ προσδεχόμενος καὶ διαδιδόμενος,
Χριστὲ ὁ Θεὸς ἡμῶν,
καὶ σοὶ τὴν δόξαν ἀναπέμπομεν,
σὺν τῷ ἀνάρχῳ σου Πατρί, καὶ τῷ παναγίῳ, καὶ ἀγαθῷ,
καὶ ζωοποιῷ σου Πνεύματι,
νῦν, καὶ ἀεί, καὶ εἰς τοὺς αἰῶνας τῶν αἰώνων. Ἀμήν.

Η ΜΕΓΑΛΗ ΕΙΣΟΔΟΣ

ΙΕΡΕΥΣ : Πάντων ἡμῶν μνησθείη Κύριος ὁ Θεὸς
ἐν τῇ βασιλείᾳ Αὐτοῦ, πάντοτε,
νῦν καὶ ἀεί, καὶ εἰς τοὺς αἰῶνας τῶν αἰώνων.

ΧΟΡΟΣ : Ἀμήν.

(Ὁ Ἱερεὺς εἰσέρχεται εἰς τὸ Ἱερὸν θέτει τὰ
Ἅγια Δῶρα ἐπάνω εἰς τὴν Ἁγίαν Τράπεζαν
καὶ τὰ θυμιάζει. Ὁ Χορὸς τελειώνει τὸ
Χερουβικόν).

ΧΟΡΟΣ : ...ταῖς ἀγγελικαῖς ἀοράτως δορυφορούμενον
[τάξεσιν.
Ἀλληλούϊα.

ΙΕΡΕΥΣ : Πληρώσωμεν τὴν δέησιν ἡμῶν τῷ Κυρίῳ.

ΧΟΡΟΣ : Κύριε ἐλέησον.

ΙΕΡΕΥΣ : Ὑπὲρ τῶν προτεθέντων τιμίων Δώρων,
τοῦ Κυρίου δεηθῶμεν.

ΧΟΡΟΣ : Κύριε ἐλέησον.

ΙΕΡΕΥΣ : Ὑπὲρ τοῦ ρυσθῆναι ἡμᾶς ἀπὸ πάσης θλίψεως,
ὀργῆς, κινδύνου καὶ ἀνάγκης,
τοῦ Κυρίου δεηθῶμεν.

ΧΟΡΟΣ : Κύριε ἐλέησον.

who receive and is received, Christ our God,
and to Thee we ascribe the glory
together with Thy Father without beginning
and Thy Holy, Good, and life-giving Spirit,
now and ever, and for evermore. Amen.

The Procession of the Gifts
(The Great Entrance) (19)

(The priest bearing the Gifts, prepared to be
offered and consecrated, comes in procession
before the Royal Gate and, turning to the people,
blesses them saying:)

PRIEST : May the Lord, our God, remember us all
[in His kingdom,
now and ever, and for evermore.
(The priest enters the sanctuary. The people or
choir conclude the Cherubic hymn:)

PEOPLE: Amen .... invisibly escorted by the Angelic
[Hosts.
Alleluia!

PRIEST : Let us complete our supplication to the
[Lord.

PEOPLE: Kyrie eleison (Lord, have mercy).

PRIEST : For these Precious Gifts here presented (20)
Let us pray to the Lord.

PEOPLE: Kyrie eleison (Lord, have mercy).

PRIEST : For our deliverance from affliction,
wrath, danger, and want,
let us implore the Lord. (21)

PEOPLE: Kyrie eleison (Lord, have mercy).

ΙΕΡΕΥΣ: (μυστικῶς)

Κύριε, ὁ Θεὸς ὁ Παντοκράτωρ, ὁ μόνος ἅγιος,
ὁ δεχόμενος θυσίαν αἰνέσεως παρὰ τῶν ἐπικαλουμένων σε
ἐν ὅλῃ καρδίᾳ,
πρόσδεξαι καὶ ἡμῶν τῶν ἁμαρτωλῶν τὴν δέησιν,
καὶ προσάγαγε τῷ ἁγίῳ σου Θυσιαστηρίῳ
καὶ ἱκάνωσον ἡμᾶς προσενεγκεῖν σοι Δῶρά τε καὶ Θυσίας
[πνευματικὰς
ὑπὲρ τῶν ἡμετέρων ἁμαρτημάτων,
καὶ τῶν τοῦ λαοῦ ἀγνοημάτων·
καὶ καταξίωσον ἡμᾶς εὑρεῖν χάριν ἐνώπιόν σου,
τοῦ γενέσθαι σοι εὐπρόσδεκτον τὴν θυσίαν ἡμῶν
καὶ ἐπισκηνῶσαι τὸ Πνεῦμα τῆς χάριτός σου τὸ ἀγαθὸν ἐφ᾽ ἡμᾶς
καὶ ἐπὶ τὰ προκείμενα Δῶρα ταῦτα
καὶ ἐπὶ πάντα τὸν λαόν σου.

ΙΕΡΕΥΣ: Ἀντιλαβοῦ, σῶσον,
ἐλέησον καὶ διαφύλαξον ἡμᾶς,
ὁ Θεός, τῇ Σῇ χάριτι.

ΧΟΡΟΣ: Κύριε ἐλέησον.

ΙΕΡΕΥΣ: Τὴν ἡμέραν πᾶσαν,
τελείαν, ἁγίαν, εἰρηνικὴν καὶ ἀναμάρτητον,
παρὰ τοῦ Κυρίου αἰτησώμεθα.

ΧΟΡΟΣ: Παράσχου Κύριε.

ΙΕΡΕΥΣ: Συγγνώμην καὶ ἄφεσιν
τῶν ἁμαρτιῶν καὶ τῶν πλημμελημάτων ἡμῶν,
παρὰ τοῦ Κυρίου αἰτησώμεθα.

PRIEST : (inaudibly)

> Lord, God, Almighty, who alone are Holy,
> Thou who accept the sacrificial offering of praise
> from those who call on Thee from the depths of
> [their hearts;
> receive also the supplication of us the sinners,
> and let it reach Thy holy altar;
> enable us to bring before Thee gifts and spiritual
> [sacrifices
> for our sins and for the sins of the people
> that have been committed in ignorance.
> Make us worthy of finding favor with Thee
> so that our Sacrifice may be well received by Thee
> and the living spirit of Thy Grace may rest on us,
> on these Gifts, and on all Thy people.

(audibly)

Help us, save us, have mercy on us, and
keep us, our God, by Thy Grace.

PEOPLE: Kyrie eleison (Lord, have mercy).

PRIEST : For a perfect, holy, peaceful, and sinless
[day,
Let us petition the Lord.

PEOPLE: Grant it, our Lord. (22)

PRIEST : For an angel of peace, a trustworthy guide,
a guardian of our souls and bodies,
let us petition the Lord.

PEOPLE: Grant it, our Lord.

PRIEST : For forgiveness and remission of our sins
[and offenses,
let us petition the Lord.

ΧΟΡΟΣ: Παράσχου Κύριε.

ΙΕΡΕΥΣ: Τὰ καλὰ καὶ συμφέροντα ταῖς ψυχαῖς ἡμῶν
καὶ εἰρήνην τῷ κόσμῳ,
παρὰ τοῦ Κυρίου αἰτησώμεθα.

ΧΟΡΟΣ: Παράσχου Κύριε.

ΙΕΡΕΥΣ: Τὸν ὑπόλοιπον χρόνον τῆς ζωῆς ἡμῶν
ἐν εἰρήνῃ καὶ μετανοίᾳ ἐκτελέσαι,
παρὰ τοῦ Κυρίου αἰτησώμεθα.

ΧΟΡΟΣ: Παράσχου Κύριε.

ΙΕΡΕΥΣ: Χριστιανὰ τὰ τέλη τῆς ζωῆς ἡμῶν,
ἀνώδυνα, ἀνεπαίσχυντα,
εἰρηνικὰ καὶ καλὴν ἀπολογίαν
τὴν ἐπὶ τοῦ φοβεροῦ Βήματος τοῦ Χριστοῦ
αἰτησώμεθα.

ΧΟΡΟΣ: Παράσχου Κύριε.

ΙΕΡΕΥΣ: Τῆς Παναγίας ἀχράντου, ὑπερευλογημένης,
ἐνδόξου Δεσποίνης ἡμῶν Θεοτόκου
καὶ ἀειπαρθένου Μαρίας
μετὰ πάντων τῶν Ἁγίων μνημονεύσαντες,
ἑαυτοὺς καὶ ἀλλήλους καὶ πᾶσαν τὴν ζωὴν
[ἡμῶν
Χριστῷ τῷ Θεῷ παραθώμεθα.

ΧΟΡΟΣ: Σοί, Κύριε.

ΙΕΡΕΥΣ: Διὰ τῶν οἰκτιρμῶν τοῦ μονογενοῦς σου Υἱοῦ,
μεθ' οὗ εὐλογητὸς εἶ,

PEOPLE: Grant it, our Lord.

PRIEST : For all that is good and beneficial to our
[souls,
and for peace in the world,
let us petition the Lord.

PEOPLE: Grant it, our Lord.

PRIEST : That we may spend the remainder of our
[lives
in peace and repentance,
let us petition the Lord.

PEOPLE: Grant it, our Lord.

PRIEST : That the end of our lives may be Christian,
without undue suffering,
without shame, peaceful;
and for a good account of ourselves
before the fearful Tribunal of Christ,
let us petition the Lord.

PEOPLE: Grant it, our Lord.

PRIEST : Let us reverently bring to mind our most
[holy,
pure, blessed and glorious Lady,
Mother of God and ever-virgin Mary with
[all the saints,
and let us commit ourselves,
one another and our whole life
to Christ our God.

PEOPLE: To Thee, our Lord.

PRIEST : Through the redeeming mercy of Thy only-
[begotten Son,
with whom Thou are blessed,

σὺν τῷ Παναγίῳ καὶ ἀγαθῷ καὶ ζωοποιῷ
[σου Πνεύματι,
νῦν, καὶ ἀεί, καὶ εἰς τοὺς αἰῶνας τῶν αἰώνων.

ΧΟΡΟΣ: Ἀμήν.

ΙΕΡΕΥΣ: Εἰρήνη πᾶσι.

ΧΟΡΟΣ: Καὶ τῷ πνεύματί σου.

ΙΕΡΕΥΣ: Ἀγαπήσωμεν ἀλλήλους,
ἵνα ἐν ὁμονοίᾳ ὁμολογήσωμεν.

ΧΟΡΟΣ: Πατέρα, Υἱὸν καὶ Ἅγιον Πνεῦμα,
Τριάδα ὁμοούσιον καὶ ἀχώριστον.

ΙΕΡΕΥΣ: Τὰς θύρας, τὰς θύρας·
ἐν σοφίᾳ πρόσχωμεν.

ΤΟ ΣΥΜΒΟΛΟΝ ΤΗΣ ΠΙΣΤΕΩΣ

ΛΑΟΣ : Πιστεύω εἰς ἕνα Θεόν, Πατέρα
Παντοκράτορα, Ποιητὴν οὐρανοῦ καὶ γῆς,
ὁρατῶν τε πάντων καὶ ἀοράτων.

Καὶ εἰς ἕνα Κύριον Ἰησοῦν Χριστόν, τὸν
Υἱὸν τοῦ Θεοῦ, τὸν μονογενῆ, τὸν ἐκ τοῦ
Πατρὸς γεννηθέντα πρὸ πάντων τῶν
αἰώνων. Φῶς ἐκ Φωτός, Θεὸν ἀληθινόν, ἐκ
Θεοῦ ἀληθινοῦ, γεννηθέντα, οὐ ποιηθέντα,
ὁμοούσιον τῷ Πατρί, δι' οὗ τὰ πάντα ἐγέ-
[νετο.

Τὸν δι' ἡμᾶς τοὺς ἀνθρώπους καὶ διὰ τὴν
ἡμετέραν σωτηρίαν, κατελθόντα ἐκ τῶν
Οὐρανῶν καὶ σαρκωθέντα ἐκ Πνεύματος
Ἁγίου καὶ Μαρίας τῆς Παρθένου, καὶ
ἐνανθρωπήσαντα.

together with the holy, righteous, and
life-giving Spirit,
now and ever, and for evermore.

PEOPLE: Amen.

PRIEST : Peace be to all.

PEOPLE: And to your spirit.

PRIEST : Let us love one another
that we may with one mind confess . . . .

PEOPLE: Father, Son, and Holy Spirit;
the Trinity, one in essence and
[inseparable. (23)

PRIEST : Guard the doors! In wisdom, let us attend!

The Creed

PEOPLE: I believe in one God, Father Almighty,
Maker of heaven and earth,
and of all things seen and unseen.
And in one Lord, Jesus Christ, the Son
[of God,
the only-begotten,
begotten of the Father before all time.
Light of light, true God of true God;
begotten not made, of the same essence with
[the Father,
through whom all things were made.
Who for us and for our salvation came down
[from heaven,
and took flesh of the Holy Spirit and the
[Virgin Mary,
and became man.

Σταυρωθέντα τε ὑπὲρ ἡμῶν ἐπὶ Ποντίου Πιλάτου, καὶ παθόντα, καὶ ταφέντα.

Καὶ ἀναστάντα τῇ τρίτῃ ἡμέρᾳ κατὰ τὰς Γραφάς.

Καὶ ἀνελθόντα εἰς τοὺς οὐρανούς, καὶ καθεζόμενον ἐκ δεξιῶν τοῦ Πατρός.

Καὶ πάλιν ἐρχόμενον μετὰ δόξης κρῖναι ζῶντας καὶ νεκρούς· οὗ τῆς Βασιλείας οὐκ ἔσται τέλος.

Καὶ εἰς τὸ Πνεῦμα τὸ Ἅγιον, τὸ Κύριον, τὸ Ζωοποιόν, τὸ ἐκ τοῦ Πατρὸς ἐκπορευόμενον, τὸ σὺν Πατρὶ καὶ Υἱῷ συμπροσκυνούμενον καὶ συνδοξαζόμενον, τὸ λαλῆσαν διὰ τῶν προφητῶν.

Εἰς Μίαν, Ἁγίαν, Καθολικὴν καὶ Ἀποστολικὴν Ἐκκλησίαν.

Ὁμολογῶ ἓν Βάπτισμα εἰς ἄφεσιν ἁμαρτιῶν.

Προσδοκῶ Ἀνάστασιν νεκρῶν·
Καὶ ζωὴν τοῦ μέλλοντος αἰῶνος.

ΧΟΡΟΣ: Ἀμήν.

ΙΕΡΕΥΣ: Στῶμεν καλῶς· στῶμεν μετὰ φόβου·
πρόσχωμεν τὴν ἁγίαν Ἀναφορὰν
ἐν εἰρήνῃ προσφέρειν.

ΧΟΡΟΣ: Ἔλεον εἰρήνης, θυσίαν αἰνέσεως.

And for us He was crucified under Pontius
                                                    [Pilate;
He suffered death, and was buried.
And on the third day He rose again
                                                    [according to
the Scriptures.
And ascended into heaven
and is seated at the right hand of the Father.
And He shall come again in glory
to judge the living and the dead,
whose kingdom shall have no end.
And in the Holy Spirit, the Sovereign, the
                                                    [giver of life.
Who proceeds from the Father,
and is worshipped and glorified
together with the Father and the Son;
who spoke through the Prophets.
In one, holy, catholic, and apostolic Church.
I acknowledge one baptism for the forgive-
                                                    [ness of sins.
I expect the resurrection of the dead;
And the life of the world to come.
Amen.

PRIEST : Let us stand reverently! Let us stand
                                                    [in awe! (24)
Let us attend that we may present
the Holy Offering in peace.

PEOPLE: Mercy, peace,   (25)
a sacrifice of praise.

ΙΕΡΕΥΣ: Ἡ χάρις τοῦ Κυρίου ἡμῶν Ἰησοῦ Χριστοῦ
καὶ ἡ ἀγάπη τοῦ Θεοῦ καὶ Πατρός,
καὶ ἡ κοινωνία τοῦ Ἁγίου Πνεύματος,
εἴη μετὰ πάντων ὑμῶν.

ΧΟΡΟΣ: Καὶ μετὰ τοῦ πνεύματός σου.

ΙΕΡΕΥΣ: Ἄνω σχῶμεν τὰς καρδίας.

ΧΟΡΟΣ: Ἔχομεν πρὸς τὸν Κύριον.

ΙΕΡΕΥΣ: Εὐχαριστήσωμεν τῷ Κυρίῳ.

ΧΟΡΟΣ: Ἄξιον καὶ δίκαιον.

ΙΕΡΕΥΣ: (μυστικῶς)

Ἄξιον καὶ δίκαιον σὲ ὑμνεῖν,
σὲ εὐλογεῖν, σὲ αἰνεῖν, σοὶ εὐχαριστεῖν, σὲ προσκυνεῖν
ἐν παντὶ τόπῳ τῆς δεσποτείας σου.
Σὺ γὰρ εἶ Θεὸς ἀνέκφραστος,
ἀπερινόητος, ἀόρατος, ἀκατάληπτος,
ἀεὶ ὢν ὡσαύτως ὤν,
σὺ καὶ ὁ μονογενής σου Υἱὸς καὶ τὸ Πνεῦμά σου τὸ ἅγιον.
Σὺ ἐκ τοῦ μὴ ὄντος εἰς τὸ εἶναι ἡμᾶς παρήγαγες
καὶ παραπεσόντας ἀνέστησας πάλιν,
καὶ οὐκ ἀπέστης πάντα ποιῶν ἕως ἡμᾶς εἰς τὸν οὐρανὸν
                                              [ἀνήγαγες
καὶ τὴν βασιλείαν σου ἐχαρίσω τὴν μέλλουσαν.
Ὑπὲρ τούτων ἁπάντων εὐχαριστοῦμέν σοι
καὶ τῷ μονογενεῖ σου Υἱῷ καὶ τῷ Πνεύματί σου τῷ ἁγίῳ·
ὑπὲρ πάντων ὧν ἴσμεν καὶ ὧν οὐκ ἴσμεν
τῶν φανερῶν καὶ ἀφανῶν εὐεργεσιῶν
τῶν εἰς ἡμᾶς γεγενημένων.
Εὐχαριστοῦμέν σοι καὶ ὑπὲρ τῆς Λειτουργίας ταύτης,
ἣν ἐκ τῶν χειρῶν ἡμῶν δέξασθαι κατηξίωσας,
καίτοι σοι παρεστήκασι χιλιάδες Ἀρχαγγέλων καὶ μυριάδες
                                              [Ἀγγέλων,

PRIEST : The Grace of our Lord Jesus Christ,
and the love of God the Father,
and the communion of the Holy Spirit,
be with you all.

PEOPLE: And with your spirit.

PRIEST : Let us lift up our hearts.

PEOPLE: We have, unto the Lord. (26)

PRIEST : Let us thank the Lord.

PEOPLE: It is proper and right.

PRIEST : (inaudibly)

It is proper and right to praise, bless, glorify,
[thank,
and worship Thee in all places of your dominion.
For Thou are God ineffable, beyond compre-
[hension,
invisible, beyond understanding,
ever-existing and always the same,
Thou and Thy only-begotten Son, and Thy
[Holy Spirit.
Thou have brought us from non-being into being,
and when we fell Thou raised us up again,
and Thou did not cease doing everything
until Thou led us to heaven and granted us
Thy kingdom to come.
For all these things we thank Thee,
and Thy only-begotten Son and Thy Holy Spirit,
for all things of which we know and
of which we do not know,
for benefits apparent and unseen
that have been bestowed upon us.
We also thank Thee for this Liturgy
which Thou have found worthy to accept
from our hands,
even though Thou are surrounded
[by thousands of Archangels,

45

τὰ Χερουβὶμ καὶ τὰ Σεραφὶμ
ἑξαπτέρυγα, πολυόμματα, μετάρσια πτερωτά,

ΙΕΡΕΥΣ : Τὸν ἐπινίκιον ὕμνον ᾄδοντα,
βοῶντα, κεκραγότα καὶ λέγοντα.

ΧΟΡΟΣ : Ἅγιος, ἅγιος, ἅγιος, Κύριος Σαβαώθ,
πλήρης ὁ οὐρανὸς καὶ ἡ γῆ τῆς δόξης Σου.
Ὡσαννὰ ἐν τοῖς ὑψίστοις·
εὐλογημένος ὁ ἐρχόμενος ἐν ὀνόματι Κυρίου.
Ὡσαννὰ ὁ ἐν τοῖς ὑψίστοις.

ΙΕΡΕΥΣ : (μυστικῶς)

Μετὰ τούτων καὶ ἡμεῖς τῶν μακαρίων Δυνάμεων,
Δέσποτα φιλάνθρωπε,
βοῶμεν καὶ λέγομεν·
Ἅγιος εἶ καὶ πανάγιος,
Σύ, καὶ ὁ μονογενής Σου Υἱὸς καὶ τὸ Πνεῦμά σου τὸ Ἅγιον.
Ἅγιος εἶ καὶ πανάγιος καὶ μεγαλοπρεπὴς ἡ δόξα σου·
ὃς τὸν κόσμον σου οὕτως ἠγάπησας,
ὥστε τὸν μονογενῆ σου Υἱὸν δοῦναι,
ἵνα πᾶς ὁ πιστεύων εἰς αὐτὸν μὴ ἀπόληται,
ἀλλ' ἔχῃ ζωὴν αἰώνιον·
ὃς ἐλθὼν καὶ πᾶσαν τὴν ὑπὲρ ἡμῶν οἰκονομίαν πληρώσας,
τῇ νυκτὶ ᾗ παρεδίδοτο,
μᾶλλον δὲ ἑαυτὸν παρεδίδου ὑπὲρ τῆς τοῦ κόσμου ζωῆς,
λαβὼν ἄρτον ἐν ταῖς ἁγίαις αὐτοῦ καὶ ἀχράντοις καὶ
[ἀμωμήτοις χερσίν,
εὐχαριστήσας καὶ εὐλογήσας, ἁγιάσας, κλάσας,
ἔδωκε τοῖς ἁγίοις αὐτοῦ Μαθηταῖς καὶ Ἀποστόλοις εἰπών·

and myriads of Angels,
by the Cherubim and Seraphim
six-winged, many-eyed, pinioned,borne aloft
[and ...

(audibly) .... singing the victory song,
proclaiming, heralding, and saying:

PEOPLE: Holy, Holy, Holy, Lord of Sabaoth,   (27)
heaven and earth are filled with Thy glory.
Praise the Lord in the highest!
Blessed is He who comes in the name of
[the Lord!

Hosanna in the highest!

PRIEST : (inaudibly)

Together with these blessed Powers, merciful
[Master,
we ourselves proclaim and say:
Holy Thou are and most Holy,
Thou and Thy only-begotten Son,
and Thy Holy Spirit.
Holy Thou are, and most Holy and sublime is
[Thy glory;
who have loved Thy world so much
that Thou gave Thy only-begotten Son
that whoever believes in Him
would not perish but have life eternal;
Who, after having come and fulfilled the divine
[plan for us,
the night He was handed over   (28)
— or rather surrendered Himself for
the life of the world —
took bread in His holy, pure, and blameless hands,
and having given thanks, He blessed it,
consecrated it, broke it,
and offered it to His holy disciples and apostles,
saying:

ΙΕΡΕΥΣ : Λάβετε, φάγετε,
τοῦτό μου ἐστι τὸ Σῶμα, τὸ ὑπὲρ ὑμῶν
[κλώμενον,
εἰς ἄφεσιν ἁμαρτιῶν.

ΧΟΡΟΣ : Ἀμήν.

ΙΕΡΕΥΣ : (μυστικῶς)

Ὁμοίως καὶ τὸ ποτήριον μετὰ τὸ δειπνῆσαι, λέγων,

ΙΕΡΕΥΣ : Πίετε ἐξ αὐτοῦ πάντες,
τοῦτό ἐστι τὸ Αἷμά μου,
τὸ τῆς Καινῆς Διαθήκης,
τὸ ὑπὲρ ὑμῶν, καὶ πολλῶν ἐκχυνόμενον,
εἰς ἄφεσιν ἁμαρτιῶν.

ΧΟΡΟΣ : Ἀμήν.

ΙΕΡΕΥΣ : (μυστικῶς)

Μεμνημένοι τοίνυν τῆς σωτηρίου ταύτης ἐντολῆς,
καὶ πάντων τῶν ὑπὲρ ἡμῶν γεγενημένων,
τοῦ Σταυροῦ, τοῦ Τάφου, τῆς Τριημέρου Ἀναστάσεως,
τῆς εἰς οὐρανοὺς Ἀναβάσεως,
τῆς ἐκ δεξιῶν Καθέδρας,
τῆς δευτέρας καὶ ἐνδόξου πάλιν Παρουσίας.

ΙΕΡΕΥΣ : (Ὑψώνει τὰ Τίμια Δῶρα)
Τὰ Σὰ ἐκ τῶν Σῶν Σοὶ προσφέρομεν,
κατὰ πάντα καὶ διὰ πάντα.

ΧΟΡΟΣ : Σὲ ὑμνοῦμεν, Σὲ εὐλογοῦμεν,
Σοὶ εὐχαριστοῦμεν, Κύριε·
καὶ δεόμεθά σου, ὁ Θεὸς ἡμῶν.

(audibly)
TAKE, EAT, THIS IS MY BODY
WHICH IS BROKEN FOR YOU,
FOR THE REMISSION OF SINS.

PEOPLE: Amen.

PRIEST : (inaudibly)
Likewise, after Supper offered the Cup saying:
(audibly)
DRINK FROM THIS ALL OF YOU;
THIS IS MY BLOOD, OF THE NEW
[TESTAMENT,
WHICH IS SHED FOR YOU AND FOR
[MANY
FOR THE REMISSION OF SINS.

PEOPLE: Amen.

PRIEST : (inaudibly)
Therefore, bringing reverently to mind
this command of our Savior
and all that came to pass for our sake;
the cross, the Tomb, the Resurrection on the
[third day,
the Ascension into heaven,
the enthronement on the right of the Father,
and the second and glorious coming,
(audibly)
Thy own of Thy own, we offer to Thee,
in all and for all   (29)

PEOPLE: We praise Thee; we bless Thee;
We give thanks to Thee, Lord,
and we implore Thee, our God.

("Ὅλοι γονατίζουν. Ὁ Ἱερεὺς προσεύχεται μυστικὰ ὅπως τὸ Ἅγιον Πνεῦμα κατέλθη ἐπὶ τὰ Τίμια Δῶρα).

ΙΕΡΕΥΣ : (μυστικῶς)

Ἔτι προσφέρομέν σοι τὴν λογικὴν ταύτην καὶ ἀναίμακτον
[λατρείαν,
καὶ παρακαλοῦμέν σε, καὶ δεόμεθα, καὶ ἱκετεύομεν.
Κατάπεμψον τὸ Πνεῦμά σου τὸ Ἅγιον ἐφ' ἡμᾶς
καὶ ἐπὶ τὰ προκείμενα Δῶρα ταῦτα.
Καὶ ποίησον τὸν μὲν Ἄρτον τοῦτον,
τίμιον Σῶμα τοῦ Χριστοῦ σου. Ἀμήν.
Τὸ δὲ ἐν τῷ Ποτηρίῳ τούτῳ,
τίμιον Αἷμα τοῦ Χριστοῦ σου. Ἀμήν.
Μεταβαλὼν τῷ Πνεύματί σου τῷ ἁγίῳ.
Ἀμήν, Ἀμήν, Ἀμήν.
Ὥστε γενέσθαι τοῖς μεταλαμβάνουσιν εἰς νῆψιν ψυχῆς,
εἰς ἄφεσιν ἁμαρτιῶν,
εἰς κοινωνίαν τοῦ ἁγίου σου Πνεύματος,
εἰς βασιλείας οὐρανῶν πλήρωμα,
εἰς παρρησίαν τὴν πρὸς σέ, μὴ εἰς κρίμα ἢ εἰς κατάκριμα.
Ἔτι προσφέρομέν σοι τὴν λογικὴν ταύτην λατρείαν
ὑπὲρ τῶν ἐν πίστει ἀναπαυσαμένων Προπατόρων,
Πατέρων, Πατριαρχῶν, Προφητῶν,
Ἀποστόλων, Κηρύκων, Εὐαγγελιστῶν,
Μαρτύρων, Ὁμολογητῶν, Ἐγκρατευτῶν,
καὶ παντὸς πνεύματος δικαίου ἐν πίστει τετελειωμένου.

ΙΕΡΕΥΣ : Ἐξαιρέτως τῆς Παναγίας ἀχράντου,
ὑπερευλογημένης, ἐνδόξου Δεσποίνης ἡμῶν

50

The Consecration

(While the people sing the above hymn
of praise, the priest proceeds with the
Consecration:)

PRIEST : (inaudibly)

Once again we offer to Thee
this spiritual and bloodless sacrificial worship, (30)
and we beg, supplicate, and beseech:
send down Thy Holy Spirit upon us
and upon these Gifts here presented.

(The priest blesses the Holy Bread:)

AND MAKE THIS BREAD THE PRECIOUS
[BODY OF YOUR CHRIST,

and that which is in this Cup

(The priest blesses the Holy Cup:)

THE PRECIOUS BLOOD OF YOUR CHRIST,

(The priest blesses both:)

CHANGING THEM BY YOUR HOLY SPIRIT.
Amen. Amen. Amen.

That they may be to those who partake of them
for vigilance of the soul, for remission of sins,
for the communion of Thy Holy Spirit,
for the fulfillment of the heavenly kingdom, (31)
for freedom to speak in The presence,
not for judgment or condemnation.
Also we offer this spiritual sacrificial worship
for those who repose in faith,
our Forefathers, Fathers, Patriarchs, Prophets,
Apostles, Preachers, Evangelists,
Martyrs, Confessors, Ascetics,
and for every righteous soul made perfect
in the Faith; (32)

(audibly)

especially, for our most holy, pure,
blessed, glorious Lady,

Θεοτόκου καὶ ἀειπαρθένου Μαρίας.

ΧΟΡΟΣ : ῎Αξιόν ἐστιν ὡς ἀληθῶς,
μακαρίζειν σε τὴν Θεοτόκον,
τὴν ἀειμακάριστον καὶ παναμώμητον
καὶ Μητέρα τοῦ Θεοῦ ἡμῶν.
Τὴν τιμιωτέραν τῶν Χερουβὶμ
καὶ ἐνδοξοτέραν ἀσυγκρίτως τῶν Σεραφίμ,
τὴν ἀδιαφθόρως Θεὸν Λόγον τεκοῦσαν,
τὴν ὄντως Θεοτόκον σὲ μεγαλύνομεν.

ΙΕΡΕΥΣ : (μυστικῶς)

Τοῦ ἁγίου ᾿Ιωάννου, ᾿Προφήτου, Προδρόμου καὶ Βαπτιστοῦ·
τῶν ἁγίων, ἐνδόξων καὶ πανευφήμων ᾿Αποστόλων·
τοῦ ῾Αγίου (τοῦ δεῖνος) οὗ καὶ τὴν μνήμην ἐπιτελοῦμεν
καὶ πάντων σου τῶν ῾Αγίων·
ὧν ταῖς ἱκεσίαις ἐπίσκεψαι ἡμᾶς ὁ Θεός.
Καὶ μνήσθητι πάντων τῶν προκεκοιμημένων
ἐπ᾿ ἐλπίδι ἀναστάσεως ζωῆς αἰωνίου (καὶ μνημονεύει οὓς
βούλεται).
Καὶ ἀνάπαυσον αὐτούς, ὁ Θεὸς ἡμῶν,
ὅπου ἐπισκοπεῖ τὸ φῶς τοῦ προσώπου σου.
῎Ετι παρακαλοῦμέν σε·
Μνήσθητι, Κύριε, πάσης ᾿Επισκοπῆς ᾿Ορθοδόξων,
τῶν ὀρθοτομούντων τὸν λόγον τῆς σῆς ἀληθείας,
παντὸς τοῦ Πρεσβυτερίου, τῆς ἐν Χριστῷ διακονίας,
καὶ παντὸς ῾Ιερατικοῦ καὶ Μοναχικοῦ τάγματος.
῎Ετι προσφέρομέν σοι τὴν λογικὴν ταύτην λατρείαν
ὑπὲρ τῆς Οἰκουμένης, ὑπὲρ τῆς ῾Αγίας, Καθολικῆς καὶ
᾿Αποστολικῆς ᾿Εκκλησίας,
ὑπὲρ τῶν ἐν ἁγνείᾳ καὶ σεμνῇ πολιτείᾳ διαγόντων,
ὑπὲρ τῶν πιστοτάτων καὶ φιλοχρίστων ἡμῶν ἀρχόντων.
Δὸς αὐτοῖς, Κύριε εἰρηνικὸν τὸ βασίλειον,
ἵνα καὶ ἡμεῖς ἐν τῇ γαλήνῃ αὐτῶν

the Mother of God and ever-virgin Mary.

PEOPLE: It is proper to bless you,
ever-esteemed Theotokos,
most pure, and Mother of our God;
more worthy of honor than the Cherubim,
and by far more glorious than the Seraphim;
you, who incorruptibly gave birth to God
[the Word,
verily Theotokos, we extoll you.
(While the above is being sung, the priest
[prays:)

PRIEST : (inaudibly)
For St. John the Prophet, Forerunner and Baptizer,
for saint . . . . whose memory we celebrate today
and for all Thy saints,
through whose supplications visit us, our God.
Be mindful of all who have died
in the hope of resurrection to an everlasting life.
(here the priest commemorates the names of
departed members of the Church)
Lay them to rest, our God,
where the light of Thy presence shines.
Furthermore, we ask Thee,
be mindful, Lord, of all Orthodox bishops
who correctly expound Thy Truth,
of all presbyters, deacons,
and of every priestly and monastic order.
We also offer this spiritual sacrifice for the whole
[world,
for Thy holy, catholic, and apostolic Church;
for those living in purity and temperance;
and for those in civil authority;
grant them, our Lord, to govern in peace
that we ourselves may in their tranquility

53

ἤρεμον καὶ ἡσύχιον βίον διάγωμεν,
ἐν πάσῃ εὐσεβείᾳ καὶ σεμνότητι·

ΙΕΡΕΥΣ : Ἐν πρώτοις μνήσθητι, Κύριε, τοῦ
Ἀρχιεπισκόπου ἡμῶν....,
ὃν χάρισαι ταῖς ἁγίαις Σου Ἐκκλησίαις ἐν
[εἰρήνῃ,
σῶον, ἔντιμον, ὑγιᾶ, μακροημερεύοντα,
καὶ ὀρθοτομοῦντα τὸν λόγον τῆς Σῆς
[ἀληθείας.

ΙΕΡΕΥΣ : (μυστικῶς)

Μνήσθητι, Κύριε, τῆς πόλεως ἐν ᾗ παροικοῦμεν
καὶ πάσης πόλεως καὶ χώρας
καὶ τῶν πίστει οἰκούντων ἐν αὐταῖς.
Μνήσθητι, Κύριε, πλεόντων, ὁδοιπορούντων,
νοσούντων, καμνόντων, αἰχμαλώτων
καὶ τῆς σωτηρίας αὐτῶν.
Μνήσθητι, Κύριε, τῶν καρποφορούντων καὶ καλλιεργούντων
ἐν ταῖς ἁγίαις σου Ἐκκλησίαις,
καὶ μεμνημένων τῶν πενήτων,
καὶ ἐπὶ πάντας ἡμᾶς τὰ ἐλέη σου ἐξαπόστειλον.

ΙΕΡΕΥΣ : Καὶ δὸς ἡμῖν ἐν ἑνὶ στόματι καὶ μιᾷ καρδίᾳ
δοξάζειν καὶ ἀνυμνεῖν τὸ πάντιμον καὶ
μεγαλοπρεπὲς ὄνομά σου,
τοῦ Πατρός, καὶ τοῦ Υἱοῦ, καὶ τοῦ Ἁγίου
[Πνεύματος,
νῦν, καὶ ἀεί, καὶ εἰς τοὺς αἰῶνας τῶν αἰώνων.

ΧΟΡΟΣ : Ἀμήν.

ΙΕΡΕΥΣ : Καὶ ἔσται τὰ ἐλέη τοῦ Μεγάλου Θεοῦ
καὶ Σωτῆρος ἡμῶν Ἰησοῦ Χριστοῦ
μετὰ πάντων ὑμῶν.

live an untroubled and serene life
in piety and temperance;

(audibly)

First of all be mindful, our Lord, of our
Archbishop . . . . . ;   (33)
grant him to Thy holy churches in peace,
safe, honorable, in health, long-lived,
and able correctly to expound the teaching
                                    [of Thy Truth.

PEOPLE: And of all Thy people.

PRIEST : (inaudibly)

Be mindful, our Lord, of the city in which we
                                    [reside,
of all cities and countries and of the faithful
who dwell in them.
Be mindful, our Lord, of those who sail,
of the sick, the suffering, the captives,
and of their salvation.
Be mindful, our Lord, of those who serve and bear
offerings to Thy holy Churches
and of those who remember the poor.
Send down Thy mercy upon us all.

(audibly)

and grant that with one voice and one heart
we may glorify and praise Thy honorable
and majestic name,
of the Father, and of the Son, and of the
                                    [Holy Spirit,
now and ever, and for evermore.

PEOPLE: Amen.

PRIEST : And the mercies of our Great God
and Savior Jesus Christ
shall be with you all.

ΧΟΡΟΣ: Καὶ μετὰ τοῦ πνεύματός σου.

ΙΕΡΕΥΣ: Πάντων τῶν Ἁγίων μνημονεύσαντες,
ἔτι καὶ ἔτι ἐν εἰρήνη τοῦ Κυρίου δεηθῶμεν.

ΧΟΡΟΣ: Κύριε ἐλέησον.

ΙΕΡΕΥΣ: Ὑπὲρ τῶν προσκομισθέντων καὶ ἁγιασθέντων
τιμίων Δώρων,
τοῦ Κυρίου δεηθῶμεν.

ΧΟΡΟΣ: Κύριε ἐλέησον.

ΙΕΡΕΥΣ: Ὅπως ὁ φιλάνθρωπος Θεὸς ἡμῶν,
ὁ προσδεξάμενος αὐτὰ εἰς τὸ ἅγιον καὶ
[ὑπερουράνιον
καὶ νοερὸν αὐτοῦ Θυσιαστήριον,
εἰς ὀσμὴν εὐωδίας πνευματικῆς,
ἀντικαταπέμψη ἡμῖν τὴν θείαν χάριν
καὶ τὴν δωρεὰν τοῦ Ἁγίου Πνεύματος,
δεηθῶμεν.

ΧΟΡΟΣ: Κύριε ἐλέησον.

ΙΕΡΕΥΣ: Ὑπὲρ τοῦ ῥυσθῆναι ἡμᾶς
ἀπὸ πάσης θλίψεως, ὀργῆς, κινδύνου καὶ
[ἀνάγκης
τοῦ Κυρίου δεηθῶμεν.

ΧΟΡΟΣ: Κύριε ἐλέησον.

ΙΕΡΕΥΣ: (μυστικῶς)

Σοὶ παρακατιθέμεθα τὴν ζωὴν ἡμῶν ἅπασαν καὶ τὴν ἐλπίδα,
Δέσποτα φιλάνθρωπε,
καὶ παρακαλοῦμέν σε, καὶ δεόμεθα καὶ ἱκετεύομεν.
Καταξίωσον ἡμᾶς μεταλαβεῖν
τῶν ἐπουρανίων σου καὶ φρικτῶν Μυστηρίων
ταύτης τῆς ἱερᾶς καὶ πνευματικῆς Τραπέζης,
μετὰ καθαροῦ συνειδότος,
εἰς ἄφεσιν ἁμαρτιῶν, εἰς συγχώρησιν πλημμελημάτων,

56

PEOPLE: And with your spirit.

PRIEST : Having made respectful mention of all the
[Saints,
let us again in peace implore the Lord.

PEOPLE: Kyrie eleison (Lord, have mercy).

PRIEST : For the precious Gifts
already offered and consecrated,
let us implore the Lord.

PEOPLE: Kyrie eleison (Lord, have mercy).

PRIEST : That our merciful God who has received
[them
at His holy, heavenly, and spiritual altar
as a savor of spiritual fragrance,
may in return send down upon us
the divine Grace and the gift of the Holy
[Spirit,
let us implore the Lord.

PEOPLE: Kyrie eleison (Lord, have mercy).

PRIEST : For our deliverance from affliction
from wrath, danger, and want,
let us implore the Lord.

PEOPLE: Kyrie eleison (Lord, have mercy).

PRIEST : (inaudibly)
To Thee we entrust, merciful Master,
our whole life and our hope,
and we beg, pray, and entreat:
render us worthy of partaking of Thy heavenly
and awesome Sacrament
of this holy and spiritual Altar
with clear conscience;
for the remission of sins,

εἰς Πνεύματος Ἁγίου κοινωνίαν,
εἰς βασιλείας οὐρανῶν κληρονομίαν,
εἰς παρρησίαν τὴν πρὸς σέ,
μὴ εἰς κρίμα, ἢ εἰς κατάκριμα.

ΙΕΡΕΥΣ : Ἀντιλαβοῦ, σῶσον, ἐλέησον
καὶ διαφύλαξον ἡμᾶς ὁ Θεὸς τῇ Σῇ χάριτι.

ΧΟΡΟΣ : Κύριε ἐλέησον.

ΙΕΡΕΥΣ : Τὴν ἡμέραν πᾶσαν, τελείαν,
ἁγίαν, εἰρηνικὴν καὶ ἀναμάρτητον,
παρὰ τοῦ Κυρίου αἰτησώμεθα.

ΧΟΡΟΣ : Παράσχου Κύριε.

ΙΕΡΕΥΣ : Ἄγγελον εἰρήνης, πιστὸν ὁδηγόν,
φύλακα τῶν ψυχῶν καὶ τῶν σωμάτων ἡμῶν,
παρὰ τοῦ Κυρίου αἰτησώμεθα.

ΧΟΡΟΣ : Παράσχου Κύριε.

ΙΕΡΕΥΣ : Συγγνώμην καὶ ἄφεσιν τῶν ἁμαρτιῶν,
καὶ τῶν πλημμελημάτων ἡμῶν,
παρὰ τοῦ Κυρίου αἰτησώμεθα.

ΧΟΡΟΣ : Παράσχου Κύριε.

ΙΕΡΕΥΣ : Τὰ καλὰ καὶ συμφέροντα ταῖς ψυχαῖς ἡμῶν,
καὶ εἰρήνην τῷ κόσμῳ,
παρὰ τοῦ Κυρίου αἰτησώμεθα.

ΧΟΡΟΣ : Παράσχου Κύριε.

ΙΕΡΕΥΣ : Τὸν ὑπόλοιπον χρόνον τῆς ζωῆς ἡμῶν,
ἐν εἰρήνῃ καὶ μετανοίᾳ ἐκτελέσαι,
παρὰ τοῦ Κυρίου αἰτησώμεθα.

ΧΟΡΟΣ : Παράσχου Κύριε.

for the forgiveness of transgressions,
for communion with the Holy Spirit,
for inheriting the kingdom of heaven;
for an unafraid presence before Thee,
not unto judgment or condemnation.
(audibly)
Help us, save us, have mercy on us,
and keep us by Thy Grace, our God.

PEOPLE: Kyrie eleison (Lord, have mercy).

PRIEST : For a perfect, holy, peaceful, and sinless
                                                            day,
let us petition the Lord.

PEOPLE: Grant it, our Lord.

PRIEST : For an angel of peace, a trustworthy guide,
a guardian of our souls and bodies,
let us petition the Lord.

PEOPLE: Grant it, our Lord.

PRIEST : For forgiveness and remission of our sins
                                                [and offenses,
let us petition the Lord.

PEOPLE: Grant it, our Lord.

PRIEST : For all that is good and profitable to our
                                                            [souls
and peace for the world,
let us petition the Lord.

PEOPLE: Grant it, our Lord.

PRIEST : That we may spend the remainder of our
                                                            [lives
in peace and penitence,
let us petition the Lord.

PEOPLE: Grant it, our Lord.

ΙΕΡΕΥΣ : Χριστιανὰ τὰ τέλη τῆς ζωῆς ἡμῶν,
ἀνώδυνα, ἀνεπαίσχυντα, εἰρηνικὰ
καὶ καλὴν ἀπολογίαν τὴν ἐπὶ τοῦ φοβεροῦ
βήματος τοῦ Χριστοῦ αἰτησώμεθα.

ΧΟΡΟΣ : Παράσχου Κύριε.

ΙΕΡΕΥΣ : Τὴν ἑνότητα τῆς πίστεως,
καὶ τὴν κοινωνίαν τοῦ Ἁγίου Πνεύματος
[αἰτησάμενοι,
ἑαυτοὺς καὶ ἀλλήλους, καὶ πᾶσαν τὴν ζωὴν
[ἡμῶν
Χριστῷ τῷ Θεῷ παραθώμεθα.

ΧΟΡΟΣ : Σοί, Κύριε.

ΙΕΡΕΥΣ : Καὶ καταξίωσον ἡμᾶς, Δέσποτα,
μετὰ παρρησίας, ἀκατακρίτως,
τολμᾶν ἐπικαλεῖσθαι Σὲ τὸν ἐπουράνιον
Θεὸν Πατέρα
καὶ λέγειν :

Η ΚΥΡΙΑΚΗ ΠΡΟΣΕΥΧΗ

ΛΑΟΣ : Πάτερ ἡμῶν, ὁ ἐν τοῖς οὐρανοῖς,
ἁγιασθήτω τὸ ὄνομά Σου·
ἐλθέτω ἡ βασιλεία Σου·
γενηθήτω τὸ θέλημά Σου ὡς ἐν οὐρανῷ
καὶ ἐπὶ τῆς γῆς.
Τὸν ἄρτον ἡμῶν τὸν ἐπιούσιον
δὸς ἡμῖν σήμερον.
Καὶ ἄφες ἡμῖν τὰ ὀφειλήματα ἡμῶν,
ὡς καὶ ἡμεῖς ἀφίεμεν τοῖς ὀφειλέταις ἡμῶν.
Καὶ μὴ εἰσενέγκῃς ἡμᾶς εἰς πειρασμόν·
ἀλλὰ ρῦσαι ἡμᾶς ἀπὸ τοῦ πονηροῦ.

PRIEST : That the end of our lives may be **Christian**,
without undue suffering,
without shame, peaceful,
and for a good account of ourselves
before the fearful Tribunal of Christ,
let us petition the Lord.

PEOPLE: Grant it, our Lord.

PRIEST : Having thus petitioned for the unity of the
[Faith
and for communion with the Holy Spirit,
let us commend ourselves, one another,
and our whole life to Christ our God.

PEOPLE: To Thee, our Lord.

PRIEST : And make us worthy, Master,
with freedom to speak and without fear of
[condemnation
to dare call upon You
the heavenly God, as Father, and say:
The Lord's Prayer

PEOPLE: Our Father in heaven,
hallowed be Thy name,
Thy kingdom come,
Thy will be done,
on earth as in heaven;
give us this day our daily bread;
and forgive us our sins
as we forgive those who sin against us;
and let us not be subjected to the test (34)
but deliver us from the evil One.   (35)

ΙΕΡΕΥΣ : Ὅτι Σοῦ ἐστὶν ἡ Βασιλεία, καὶ ἡ δύναμις καὶ
[ἡ δόξα,
τοῦ Πατρός, καὶ τοῦ Υἱοῦ, καὶ τοῦ Ἁγίου
[Πνεύματος,
νῦν, καὶ ἀεί, καὶ εἰς τοὺς αἰῶνας τῶν αἰώνων.
ΧΟΡΟΣ : Ἀμήν.
ΙΕΡΕΥΣ : Εἰρήνη πᾶσι.
ΧΟΡΟΣ : Καὶ τῷ πνεύματί σου.
ΙΕΡΕΥΣ : Τὰς κεφαλὰς ἡμῶν τῷ Κυρίῳ κλίνωμεν.
ΧΟΡΟΣ : Σοί, Κύριε.
ΙΕΡΕΥΣ : (μυστικῶς)

Εὐχαριστοῦμέν σοι, Βασιλεῦ ἀόρατε,
ὁ τῇ ἀμετρήτῳ σου δυνάμει τὰ πάντα δημιουργήσας,
καὶ τῷ πλήθει τοῦ ἐλέους σου ἐξ οὐκ ὄντων
εἰς τὸ εἶναι τὰ πάντα παραγαγών.
Αὐτός, Δέσποτα,
οὐρανόθεν ἔπιδε ἐπὶ τοὺς ὑποκεκλικότας σοι τὰς ἑαυτῶν
[κεφαλάς·
οὐ γὰρ ἔκλιναν σαρκὶ καὶ αἵματι,
ἀλλὰ σοὶ τῷ φοβερῷ Θεῷ.
Σὺ οὖν, Δέσποτα,
τὰ προκείμενα πᾶσιν ἡμῖν εἰς ἀγαθὸν ἐξομάλισον
κατὰ τὴν ἑκάστου ἰδίαν χρείαν·
τοῖς πλέουσι σύμπλευσον·
τοῖς ὁδοιποροῦσι συνόδευσον·
τοὺς νοσοῦντας ἴασαι, ὁ ἰατρὸς τῶν ψυχῶν καὶ τῶν σωμάτων
[ἡμῶν.

ΙΕΡΕΥΣ : Χάριτι, καὶ οἰκτιρμοῖς, καὶ φιλανθρωπίᾳ
τοῦ Μονογενοῦς Σου Υἱοῦ,
μεθ' οὗ εὐλογητὸς εἶ, σὺν τῷ παναγίῳ,
καὶ ἀγαθῷ, καὶ ζωοποιῷ Σου Πνεύματι,
νῦν, καὶ ἀεί, καὶ εἰς τοὺς αἰῶνας τῶν αἰώνων.

PRIEST : For Thine is the kingdom, and the power,
[and the glory,
now and ever, and for evermore.

PEOPLE: Amen.

PRIEST : Peace be with all.

PEOPLE: And with your spirit.

PEOPLE: Let us bow our heads to the Lord.

PEOPLE: To Thee, our Lord.

PRIEST : (inaudibly)
We give thanks to Thee, invisible King,
who by Thy infinite power have created all things
and in Thy great mercy have brought all things
from non-being into being.
Thou, Master, do now also look down from
[heaven (36)
upon those who have bowed their heads before
[Thee;
they have bowed not before flesh and blood,
but before Thee, awesomely mighty God.
Therefore, Lord, administer these Gifts for our
[good
according to each one's particular needs;
stand by those who sail the seas,
be a companion to those who travel by land or air.
Heal the sick, the healer of our souls and bodies.
(audibly)
By the Grace, mercy, and love for us
of Thy only-begotten Son
with whom Thou are blessed
together with Thy all-holy, good and life-
[giving Spirit,
now and ever, and for evermore.

ΧΟΡΟΣ: Ἀμήν.

ΙΕΡΕΥΣ: (μυστικῶς)

Πρόσχες, Κύριε Ἰησοῦ Χριστέ, ὁ Θεὸς ἡμῶν,
ἐξ ἁγίου κατοικητηρίου σου καὶ ἀπὸ θρόνου δόξης τῆς
[βασιλείας σου
καὶ ἐλθὲ εἰς τὸ ἁγιάσαι ἡμᾶς,
ὁ ἄνω τῷ Πατρὶ συγκαθήμενος
καὶ ὧδε ἡμῖν ἀοράτως συνών·
καὶ καταξίωσον τῇ κραταιᾷ σου χειρὶ
μεταδοῦναι ἡμῖν τοῦ ἀχράντου Σώματός σου καὶ τοῦ τιμίου
[Αἵματος,
καὶ δι᾽ ἡμῶν παντὶ τῷ λαῷ.

ΙΕΡΕΥΣ: Πρόσχωμεν.
Τὰ Ἅγια τοῖς ἁγίοις!

ΧΟΡΟΣ: Εἷς Ἅγιος,
εἷς Κύριος,
Ἰησοῦς Χριστός,
εἰς δόξαν Θεοῦ Πατρός. Ἀμήν.

ΚΟΙΝΩΝΙΚΟΝ

ΧΟΡΟΣ: Αἰνεῖτε τὸν Κύριον ἐκ τῶν Οὐρανῶν.
Ἀλληλούϊα. (τρὶς)

(Ψαλλομένου τοῦ Κοινωνικοῦ ὁ Ἱερεὺς μετα-
λαμβάνει τῶν Ἀχράντων Μυστηρίων. Μετὰ
ταῦτα ἀναγινώσκει τὴν ἀκόλουθον εὐχήν:)

PEOPLE: Amen.

PRIEST : (inaudibly)

Favor us with Thy attention, Lord Christ our God,
from Thy holy dwelling and from the glorious
                                            [throne
of Thy kingdom,
and come to sanctify us,
Thou who sit above with the Father
yet are here invisibly with us;
and deem it worthy to impart to us
by Thy mighty hand
— and through us to all the people —
Thy sacred Body and Thy precious Blood.   (37)

PRIEST : (audibly)

Let us attend!
The holy Gifts for the holy people
of God.   (38)

PEOPLE: One alone is Holy,
         one is the Lord,
         Jesus Christ,
         for the glory of God the Father. Amen.
         (Communion hymn)
         Praise the Lord from the heavens,
         praise Him in the highest!
         Alleluia!

Communion

(While the above hymn is sung, the priest
receives Holy Communion at the completion
of which he gives thanks as follows:

ΙΕΡΕΥΣ: (μυστικῶς)

Εὐχαριστοῦμεν σοι, Δέσποτα φιλάνθρωπε,
Εὐεργέτα τῶν ψυχῶν ἡμῶν,
ὅτι καὶ τῇ παρούσῃ ἡμέρᾳ
κατηξίωσας ἡμᾶς τῶν ἐπουρανίων σου καὶ ἀθανάτων
Μυστηρίων·
ὀρθοτόμησον ἡμῶν τὴν ὁδόν,
στήριξον ἡμᾶς ἐν τῷ φόβῳ σου τοὺς πάντας,
φρούρησον ἡμῶν τὴν ζωήν,
ἀσφάλισαι ἡμῶν τὰ διαβήματα,
εὐχαῖς καὶ ἱκεσίαις τῆς ἐνδόξου Θεοτόκου καὶ ἀειπαρθένου
[Μαρίας
καὶ πάντων τῶν Ἁγίων σου.

(Εἰς τὸ τέλος τοῦ κοινωνικοῦ ἐξέρχεται
κρατῶν τὸ Ἅγιον Ποτήριον καὶ λέγει):

ΙΕΡΕΥΣ: Μετὰ φόβου Θεοῦ,
πίστεως καὶ ἀγάπης
προσέλθετε.   (Οἱ πιστοὶ κοινωνοῦν. Μετὰ ταῦτα):

ΙΕΡΕΥΣ: Σῶσον ὁ Θεὸς τὸν λαόν Σου
καὶ εὐλόγησον τὴν κληρονομίαν Σου.

ΧΟΡΟΣ: Εἴδομεν τὸ φῶς τὸ ἀληθινόν,
ἐλάβομεν Πνεῦμα ἐπουράνιον,
εὕρομεν πίστιν ἀληθῆ,
ἀδιαίρετον Τριάδα προσκυνοῦντες.
Αὕτη γὰρ ἡμᾶς ἔσωσεν.

ΙΕΡΕΥΣ: (μυστικῶς)

Ὑψώθητι ἐπὶ τοὺς οὐρανούς, ὁ Θεός,
καὶ ἐπὶ πᾶσαν τὴν γῆν ἡ δόξα σου (τρὶς)
Εὐλογητὸς ὁ Θεὸς ἡμῶν....

ΙΕΡΕΥΣ: πάντοτε, νῦν καὶ ἀεὶ καὶ εἰς τοὺς αἰῶνας τῶν
[αἰώνων.

66

PRIEST : (inaudibly)

We thank Thee, merciful Master and benefactor
of our souls,
that once more Thou have made us worthy of
and immortal Sacrament;   [Thy heavenly
make straight our path,
make us all strong in Thy fear;
watch over our life, make our endeavors safe;
through the prayers and supplications
of the glorious Mother of God and ever-virgin
and of all Thy Saints.   [Mary

(Then he comes to the Royal Gate with the
                                    [Chalice).

PRIEST : With the fear of God,
with faith and with love,
draw near!

(Holy Communion is imparted to the faithful.
Then the priest raises the Chalice and blesses
the people:)

PRIEST : Save Thy people, our God,
and bless Thy inheritance.

PEOPLE: We have seen the true Light;
we have received the heavenly Spirit;
we have found the true faith
worshipping the undivided Trinity;
for this has saved us.

PRIEST : (Blessing the people with the Holy Gifts:)
(inaudibly)

Be exalted, our God, above the Heavens
and Thy glory may prevail over the whole world.
Blessed be our God . . . . .   (Three times)

(audibly)
now, and ever, and for evermore.

ΧΟΡΟΣ: Ἀμήν.

ΙΕΡΕΥΣ: Ὀρθοί·
μεταλαβόντες τῶν θείων, ἁγίων
ἀχράντων, ἀθανάτων, ἐπουρανίων
καὶ ζωοποιῶν, φρικτῶν τοῦ Χριστοῦ
                       [Μυστηρίων,
ἀξίως εὐχαριστήσωμεν τῷ Κυρίῳ.
Ἀντιλαβοῦ, σῶσον,
ἐλέησον καὶ διαφύλαξον ἡμᾶς, ὁ Θεός,
τῇ Σῇ χάριτι.
Τὴν ἡμέραν πᾶσαν, τελείαν, ἁγίαν,
εἰρηνικὴν καὶ ἀναμάρτητον αἰτησάμενοι
ἑαυτοὺς καὶ ἀλλήλους καὶ πᾶσαν τὴν ζωὴν
                       [ἡμῶν
Χριστῷ τῷ Θεῷ παραθώμεθα.

ΧΟΡΟΣ: Σοί, Κύριε.

ΙΕΡΕΥΣ: Ὅτι Σὺ εἶ ὁ ἁγιασμὸς ἡμῶν
καὶ Σοὶ τὴν δόξαν ἀναπέμπομεν,
τῷ Πατρί, καὶ τῷ Υἱῷ, καὶ τῷ Ἁγίῳ Πνεύματι,
νῦν, καὶ ἀεί, καὶ εἰς τοὺς αἰῶνας τῶν αἰώνων.

ΧΟΡΟΣ: Ἀμήν.

ΙΕΡΕΥΣ: Ἐν εἰρήνῃ προέλθωμεν.
Τοῦ Κυρίου δεηθῶμεν.

ΧΟΡΟΣ: Κύριε ἐλέησον.

ΙΕΡΕΥΣ: Ὁ εὐλογῶν τοὺς εὐλογοῦντας Σε, Κύριε,
καὶ ἁγιάζων τοὺς ἐπὶ Σοὶ πεποιθότας,
σῶσον τὸν λαόν Σου καὶ εὐλόγησον
τὴν κληρονομίαν Σου.

PEOPLE: Amen.

PRIEST : Let us stand!
Having partaken of the divine, holy, pure,
[immortal,
heavenly, life-giving and awesome
[Sacrament of Christ,
let us worthily give thanks to the Lord. (39)
Help us, save us, have mercy on us,
and keep us by Thy Grace, our God.
Having petitioned for the whole day to be
[perfect,
holy, peaceful, and sinless,
let us commend ourselves, one another,
and our whole life to Christ our God.

PEOPLE: To Thee, our Lord.

PRIEST : For Thou are our sanctification
and to Thee we ascribe glory,
to the Father, and to the Son,
and to the Holy Spirit,
now and ever, and for evermore.

PEOPLE: Amen.

PRIEST : Let us depart in peace!
Let us implore the Lord.

PEOPLE: Kyrie eleison (Lord, have mercy).

PRIEST : Thou who bless those who bless Thee,
[our Lord,
who sanctify those who put their trust
[in Thee,
save Thy people and bless Thy inheritance;

Τὸ πλήρωμα τῆς Ἐκκλησίας Σου φύλαξον,
ἁγίασον τοὺς ἀγαπῶντας τὴν εὐπρέπειαν
[τοῦ οἴκου Σου.
Σὺ αὐτοὺς ἀντιδόξασον τῇ θεϊκῇ Σου δυνάμει
καὶ μὴ ἐγκαταλίπῃς ἡμᾶς τοὺς ἐλπίζοντας
[ἐπὶ Σέ.

Εἰρήνην τῷ κόσμῳ Σου δώρησαι,
ταῖς Ἐκκλησίαις Σου,
τοῖς Ἱερεῦσι,
τοῖς ἄρχουσιν ἡμῶν,
τῷ στρατῷ καὶ παντὶ τῷ λαῷ Σου.
Ὅτι πᾶσα δόσις ἀγαθὴ καὶ πᾶν δώρημα
[τέλειον
ἄνωθέν ἐστι καταβαῖνον
ἐκ Σοῦ τοῦ Πατρὸς τῶν φώτων·
καὶ Σοὶ τὴν δόξαν καὶ εὐχαριστίαν
καὶ προσκύνησιν ἀναπέμπομεν,
τῷ Πατρί, καὶ τῷ Υἱῷ, καὶ τῷ ἁγίῳ Πνεύματι,
νῦν, καὶ ἀεί, καὶ εἰς τοὺς αἰῶνας τῶν αἰώνων.

ΧΟΡΟΣ: Ἀμήν.
Εἴη τὸ ὄνομα Κυρίου εὐλογημένον
ἀπὸ τοῦ νῦν καὶ ἕως τοῦ αἰῶνος. (τρὶς)

ΙΕΡΕΥΣ: (μυστικῶς)

Τὸ πλήρωμα τοῦ Νόμου καὶ τῶν προφητῶν
αὐτὸς ὑπάρχων, Χριστὲ ὁ Θεὸς ἡμῶν,
ὁ πληρώσας πᾶσαν Πατρικὴν οἰκονομίαν,
πλήρωσον χαρᾶς καὶ εὐφροσύνης τὰς καρδίας ἡμῶν
πάντοτε, νῦν καὶ ἀεὶ καὶ εἰς τοὺς αἰῶνας τῶν αἰώνων. Ἀμήν.

preserve the entire body of **Thy Church;** (40)
sanctify those who lovingly work for the
beauty of Thy House,
glorify them in return by Thy divine power,
and do not forsake us who hope in Thee.
Grant peace to Thy world,
to Thy Churches,
to the clergy,
to our authorities,
and to all Thy people.
For, every good grant and every perfect gift
comes from above,
from Thee the Father of Light;
and to Thee we ascribe glory,
and offer thanks and worship,
to the Father,
and to the Son,
and to the Holy Spirit,
now, and ever, and for evermore.

PEOPLE: Amen.

Blessed be the name of the Lord;
from this time forth
and for evermore. (Three times)

PRIEST : (inaudibly)

Being the fulfillment of the law and the Prophets,
Christ our God,
Thou who fulfilled the dispensation of the Father,
fill our hearts with joy and gladness,
now, and ever, and for evermore. Amen.

ΑΠΟΛΥΣΙΣ

ΙΕΡΕΥΣ : Τοῦ Κυρίου δεηθῶμεν.

ΧΟΡΟΣ : Κύριε ἐλέησον. (τρὶς)
Πάτερ ἅγιε, εὐλόγησον.

ΙΕΡΕΥΣ : Εὐλογία Κυρίου καὶ ἔλεος
ἔλθοι ἐφ' ὑμᾶς,
τῇ Αὐτοῦ θείᾳ χάριτι καὶ φιλανθρωπίᾳ,
[πάντοτε,
νῦν, καὶ ἀεί, καὶ εἰς τοὺς αἰῶνας τῶν αἰώνων.

ΧΟΡΟΣ : Ἀμήν.

ΙΕΡΕΥΣ : Δόξα σοι Χριστὲ ὁ Θεός,
ἡ ἐλπὶς ἡμῶν, δόξα Σοι.
(Ὁ ἀναστὰς ἐκ νεκρῶν) Χριστὸς ὁ ἀληθινὸς
Θεὸς ἡμῶν,
ταῖς πρεσβείαις τῆς παναχράντου
καὶ παναμώμου ἁγίας αὐτοῦ Μητρός·
δυνάμει τοῦ τιμίου καὶ ζωοποιοῦ Σταυροῦ·
προστασίαις τῶν τιμίων ἐπουρανίων
Δυνάμεων ἀσωμάτων·
ἱκεσίαις τοῦ τιμίου, ἐνδόξου Προφήτου,
Προδρόμου καὶ Βαπτιστοῦ Ἰωάννου·
τῶν ἁγίων ἐνδόξων καὶ πανευφήμων
[Ἀποστόλων.
τῶν ἁγίων ἐνδόξων καὶ καλλινίκων μαρτύρων·
τῶν ὁσίων καὶ θεοφόρων Πατέρων ἡμῶν·
τῶν ἁγίων καὶ δικαίων Θεοπατόρων
Ἰωακεὶμ καὶ Ἄννης·

Dismissal

PRIEST : Let us implore the Lord.

PEOPLE: Kyrie eleison (Lord, have mercy).

PRIEST : (blessing the people)
May the blessing and mercy of the Lord
always come upon you through His divine
[Grace and Love,
now, and ever, and for evermore.

PEOPLE: Amen.

PRIEST : Glory to Thee, Christ our God and
[our hope, (41)
Glory to Thee!
May the risen Christ,
our true God,
—through the intercessions of His most pure
and holy Mother;
through the power of the precious and
life-giving Cross;
through the protection of the heavenly
spiritual Powers;
through the supplications of the Forerunner
John the Baptist;
of the holy glorious and praiseworthy
[Apostles;
of the holy, glorious, and victorious martyrs;
of the saintly and divine ancestors Joachim
[and Anna;

τοῦ Ἁγίου (τῆς ἡμέρας), οὗ καὶ τὴν μνήμην
[ἐπιτελοῦμεν
καὶ πάντων τῶν Ἁγίων,
ἐλεῆσαι καὶ σῶσαι ἡμᾶς, ὡς ἀγαθὸς καὶ
φιλάνθρωπος, καὶ ἐλεήμων Θεός.

Δι' εὐχῶν τῶν ἁγίων Πατέρων ἡμῶν,
Κύριε Ἰησοῦ Χριστέ, ὁ Θεὸς ἡμῶν,
ἐλέησον καὶ σῶσον ἡμᾶς.

ΧΟΡΟΣ: Ἀμήν.

(Ἐπακολουθεῖ ἡ διανομὴ τοῦ ἀντιδώρου).

74

of Saint . . . . . (of the church);
of Saint . . . . whose memory we celebrate;
and of all the saints—
have mercy on us and save us
being a Good, man-loving, and merciful
[God.
LORD JESUS CHRIST, OUR GOD,
HAVE MERCY ON US,
THROUGH THE PRAYERS OF OUR
[HOLY FATHERS.

PEOPLE: Amen.
(Antidoron is distributed while appropriate
hymns are sung)

THE END

(Give Glory to God)

NOTES ON THE TEXT

1. The Greek βασιλεία primarily means the region or country governed by a king, a *kingdom, realm*. Ἡ βασιλεία τοῦ Θεοῦ, τοῦ Χριστοῦ, denote more authority than spatial extension (St. Matthew 9:35; 10:7; et. al. Romans 14:17). In the Liturgy, βασιλεία obviously refers, in the first place, to *kingly power, authority, dominion, reign.* However, this reference appears to accept a double interpretation. Βασιλεία may be taken to refer to a present-day state of God's rule as well as to a state hereafter, eschatological. Of the two most recent and best English translations — The New English Bible (1970), and The New American Bible (1970) — the first refers to βασιλεία as *kingdom,* the second as *reign.* We have reluctantly retained *kingdom* because, besides its spatial meaning it could be taken in a metaphorical sense as well, and because it has become so familiar to people through King James' and subsequent translations.

The Greek εἰς τοὺς αἰῶνας τῶν αἰώνων, has been rendered in English with some pleonasms that can duplicate neither the resonance of the Greek nor its vivid imagery of motion through time. Then, the English sounds so idiomatic as to be unrecognizable even by people with college training in the language. *For evermore*, seems to adequately convey the sense and at the same time to hint to a βασιλεία perpetually ruling over the whole existence.

2. Τοῦ Κυρίου δεηθῶμεν, definitely has varying meanings throughout the Liturgy. Invariably translating it with *Let us pray to the Lord*, appears to deprive the text of certain fine but just as important distinctions that point out to the true nature of each prayer which it prefaces. Δέομαι, fundamentally means *to be in want, to need, to ask, to request*; it is so used in Matthew 9:38; Luke 5:12; 8:28,38; and elsewhere; it also means *to pray, offer prayer, beseech, supplicate, entreat*, Luke 21:36; 22:32; Acts 4:31; 8:22,24; and elsewhere.

Obviously, a correct rendering into English will have to be in harmony with the contents of the prayer which it opens. If the text following it, is a straight prayer referring to spiritual more than to mundane supplication, the English *let us pray* would be correct. But in this case, we have a series of petitions relating to as spiritual a reality as *the peace from heaven* and as mundane a reality as the weather and the fruiting of the earth. While we cannot deny the legitimacy of these mundane supplications as elements of true prayer, their petitionary nature is too obvious to be overlooked. And because δέομαι contains the

77

element of a *de profundis* request bordering the awe of a spiritually absolute discourse with God, we can qualify the request with, *in prayer.* Thus, an equally acceptable rendering would be, *let us in prayer ask of the Lord.*

3. Καὶ τῆς τῶν πάντων ἐνώσεως, does not — at least on points of language — mean for the union of all Churches, nor can we leave it unqualified, as some translators have, with *for the union of all;* πάντων is unmistakably of masculine gender, genitive of the plural, and means of all ἀνθρώπων. The opinion that it could mean *of all things,* since πάντων could be of neuter gender as well, is too philosophical and lacks Biblical or Patristic support. Perhaps, the ultimate meaning is *of all Churches,* since union of all people will bring about the union of all Churches.

4. *Laity* is a derivation from the Greek λαὸς and, in spite of its rather sharp distinction from the *clergy* which it has aquired through the ages, we should understand it in the Orthodox connotation of its being not the inferior to clergy element in the Church, rather its equal and indispensable complement to constituting the sacramental reality of the Church of Christ.

5. εὐκρασίας ἀέρων, does not mean *favorable winds.'* Ἀὴρ is not wind, as in modern Greek. It denotes the lower atmospheric levels

where temperature currents result in producing one kind of weather or another.

Καὶ καιρῶν εἰρηνικῶν, is translated by every single translator with *for peaceful times*. Καιρὸς is the *season* rather than *time*, which is denoted by χρόνος. So, *peaceful times* should be changed to *temperate seasons*.

6. Τῆς σωτηρίας αὐτῶν, does not completely cover all the classes to which the petition refers. It seems that σωτηρία is used to include safety and/or deliverance. Safety would better apply to travelers, deliverance to sick and prisoners. Of course, σωτηρία — salvation, would crown all. Perhaps, *safety and salvation*, would make the meaning of the text more complete.

7. Πάσης θλίψεως, means, *all kinds of affliction-distress*. But the collective singular *affliction* would do well without involving the meaning further, so much so that some consider what follows — wrath, danger, and want — kinds of affliction, and, perhaps, with good reason.

8. Ἀντιλαβοῦ, means *help us* only in the last analysis. Its graphic expression is, *take us in turn (extend your protection)*, and, perhaps, *in return* for our surrendering ourselves to You.

9. Μνημονεύσαντες, has been in most translations exchanged for *commemorating*. First, the tense of the verb is not in the present but in the past (actually past participle), that is,

having already done so. Of course, we have not commemorated up to this point in the Liturgy. Various explanations have been advanced for this past participle. None can be justified from the text. The past tense is either a grammatical error, or merely an invitation on the part of the celebrant for the congregation to effect the commemoration now, and then to commend themselves to Christ, as the text requires further down. The first instance in which this type of commemoration is mentioned in the more ancient Liturgy of St. James, the verb is μνημονεύσωμεν instead of μνημονεύσαντες, that is, *let us respectfully call to mind* . . . instead of *having called to mind*, an act which we have not effected up to this point in the Liturgy. This seems to be the most probable explanation without requiring, as the others do, evidence of doubtful validity from without the Liturgy.

Then, *commemorating*, does not convey the simplicity and directness of the Greek. *Commemorating* is a Latin rendering, meaning *bringing intensely to mind*. But owing to its long association with Latin liturgical practices, it has acquired connotations that go beyond the original calling of the celebrant to *respectfully mention* the names of the virgin-Mary and the rest of the Saints. *Commemorating* carries a doctrinal crust that the Greek μνημονεύσαντες never assumed in the course of time in the East. Thus, it should be avoided, at least in cases where honor is clearly intended rather than dogmatical coloring regarding the virgin-Mary and the Saints.

10. Σοὶ Κύριε. *To Thee, our Lord*, should be sung slowly so that the celebrant will have time to read the inaudible prayer that follows, and which belongs there and not to the time when the *antiphon* is sung.

11. Τὸ πλήρωμα τῆς ἐκκλησίας σου, means *the entire membership of Your Church.* If *fullness of Thy Church*, as used by other translators, is meant to include the membership of the universal Church of Christ, then it does convey the intended meaning. But how would the reader know? We prefer the more prosaic and more accurate *all the members* instead of *the fullness.*

12. This hymn is traditionally ascribed to Justinian. Whoever its author, the hymn is a perfect example of doctrinal poetry that served a double purpose during the time the Church was in the process of formulating her Christological position in the midst of—often hopelessly — confused and confusing heretical teachings: that is, to provide a moving prayer format for common worship and to declare through it beliefs that gradually were incorporated into what is today known as Orthodox dogmatics.

13. Θανάτῳ θάνατον πατήσας, means *trampling death by death,* as is often quoted, only literally. The meaning from other Patristic usage points out to *contemptibly doing away with* (Chrys. hom. 11.2 in Col. (11,407) F). Again, we prefer the less picturesque but more meaningful *destroying.*

14. Ἀπολυτίκιον, is rightly translated as *Dismissal hymn.* Yet, the meaning is not one of dismissal but of crowning the service and thus of closing it with this hymn. Invariably, this hymn is of the nature of a personal anthem, as it were, relating to the virgin-Mary or to one of the Saints, or of a poem giving the essence and the teaching of one of those particular feasts, known in Greek as Δεσποτικαὶ ἑορταί, devoted to the events of our Lord's earthly life.

15. This is the first procession in the Liturgy and is called in Greek Μικρὰ Εἴσοδος, obviously in distinction to the Μεγάλη Εἴσοδος that comes later on and during which the priest comes out of the sanctuary (from the northern door, provided the altar faces east) and reenters it through the middle or Royal Gate holding the Gifts to be offered for consecration.

In this first procession, the priest comes out with the Gospel, stands before the Royal Gate, raises the Gospel and proclaims it to be the book of wisdom, that is, of divine wisdom.

Originally, though, the deacon with the priest brought in procession the book of the Gospels from the vestry where it was kept under lock and key from fear of being stolen or desecrated by fanatic pagans or heretics. Obviously, they made their entrance into the sanctuary proper through the Royal Gate before which they would pause, the deacon would ask the people to stand reverently, and raising the Book high so that everybody could see it, he proclaimed it to contain the Word of God. From this Book, both the baptized members as well as the catechumens (the candidates for baptism in the course of being instructed) would later in the Liturgy be edified and spiritually strengthened. It is logical to assume that the deacon or priest holding the Gospel would face the people, and after raising it he would bless the people with it. Thus, he would not be facing the altar as is the practice today. Some Orthodox Churches, though, have retained the obviously ancient practice of making the proclamation of Wisdom facing the people. This procession is called by some translators *Little Entrance,* in a verbatim translation of the Greek rubric. But even the Greek Μικρὰ Εἴσοδος, does not signify the meaning of the procession. Needless to say, the English *Little Entrance* is completely meaningless and can be misconstrued for anything else but for that which the procession seems to signify. (See extensive discussion of Little Entrance in Part II, p. 278). After studying many possible choices, we decided to stay with a simple designation of what is physically taking place instead of trying to explain by way of a title the meaning of the procession. The proclamation of the celebrant, *Wisdom! Let us stand!* is sufficiently self-explanatory, if the words are clearly enunciated and not slaughtered in an attempt, on the part of the celebrant, to balance his voice on the Byzantine musical precipices.

16. The Greek ὁ ἐν ἁγίοις ἀναπαυόμενος, is difficult to translate and make sense for the average worshipper who is ignorant of the finer folds of theological contemplation. The Greek ἀναπαύομαι means *to rest,* and many translations have, *who rest in the saints.* How God can rest in the saints or among the saints is difficult to understand. The meaning is not one of *rest* or *repose* but one of *dwelling* in the saints or among the saints. This is clearly borne out by consistent Patristic usage of the term in the spiritual meaning of God *dwelling in man:* οὐκ ἄρα ἐπιθυμήσει τινὸς ἑτέρου ὁ ἔχων ἀναπαυόμενον τὸν Θεόν, (Clem. Str. 7.13 p. 58.32;M.9.516A) and many others.

17. After the rubric relating to the reading of the appointed Gospel passage, even the later editions of the Greek Liturgy still reprint a num-

ber of inaudible prayers and audible admonitions addressed to the catechumens who at the end of this series of prayers were called by the deacon or celebrant to leave the church as being not yet fully initiated by baptism. The remaining of the Liturgy, including, of course, Consecration and Communion, was exclusively reserved for the baptized members of the Church, and was called the Liturgy of the Faithful. This, in distinction to the part up to this point — including the Epistle, the Gospel, and the sermon — which was known as the Liturgy of the Catechumens. Today, these prayers bear only historical significance and, as a rule, are omitted. If the Orthodox Church ever undertakes a large scale missionary work and finds herself with a class of people of the category of catechumens, these prayers might again come to life. But even in this eventuality, the reintroduction of these prayers is doubtful considering the fact that we do not keep our catechumens today in the stage of preparation but only for as long as it takes them to verse themselves in the fundamentals of our dogmatics and practices. This period might be limited to a few weeks or even a few days, seeing that we deal today with schooled people who can even instruct themselves by studying on levels of religious understanding that few could at the time of the composition of the Liturgy attain, even among the clergy.

In all probability, the prayers for the catechumens will remain as specimen of liturgical antiquity, regrettable victims to ever changing religious realities, so much so that two or three of these are from among the best in the Liturgy.

The omission of these prayers has created a sequential problem that celebrants should correct. After the reading of the Gospel, usually the celebrant makes the pronouncement, ὅπως ὑπὸ τοῦ κράτους σου... *that we may ever being protected by Thy power* . . . But this by itself does not make sense since it is the audible pronouncement of an inaudible prayer, the last before the Liturgy of the Faithful begins with the Cherubic Hymn. Actually, it is a preparatory prayer for celebrating the bloodless sacrifice later on. After the reading of the Gospel, the choir or congregation should sing the, *Glory to Thee, our Lord, glory to Thee!* slowly so as to give the priest time to read inaudibly the prayer, *Again and oftentimes* . . .

18. **Ζωοποιῷ Τριάδι,** is literally, *to the life-creating Trinity*. Life giving means the same in a more familiar and more understandable linguistic frame of English.

19. This second and more elaborate procession, with the celebrant bringing the unconsecrated Gifts from the preparation conch (Prothesis)

to the sanctuary through the Royal Gate to be laid on the altar proper, is known in Greek as the Μεγάλη Εἴσοδος. With little attention as to its meaning, this has been translated into English as the *Great Entrance,* in distinction to the *Little Entrance* previously discussed. We have decided to title this procession according to its function so as to make sense for the worshipper or the student of the Liturgy. Worshippers should bear in mind that the Gifts carried by the priest are not the Sanctified Gifts, that is, the Body and Blood of Christ, but only the elements of bread and wine prepared to be offered to God for consecration later on in the Liturgy. Thus, though the congregation should visually follow this procession with extreme reverence, they should keep in mind that the Gifts borne by the celebrant are not the Body and Blood of Christ as it is believed by many in line with an erroneous tradition deriving from some of the Orthodox countries of Europe. It is unfortunate that the Liturgy does not provide for a later procession with the Sanctified Gifts through the congregation for the purpose of bringing into physical proximity the sacramental Christ with His mystical body, the believers, and for thereby sanctifying them. The mistaking of the unconsecrated Gifts for the Sanctified Gifts on the part of the people clearly shows that they would highly value the bringing *down* to them the sacramental Christ in the passing of Whom they could bend both their knees and their hearts.

20. The Greek προτεθέντων means, that have been placed here before something or someone. In this case, the Gifts rest on the altar before God to be offered for Consecration at the proper time of the Liturgy.

21. The meaning here requires changing of *pray* to *implore*.

22. The Greek Παράσχου Κύριε, loses a great deal in any possible translation. In Greek, it needs no pronoun to refer to the petition before it. *Grant it,* or *Grant this,* are both lacking the impact of the Greek unappended verb. Then, Κύριε, is always used in Greek without the possessive pronoun *our* or *my,* although the possessive is invariably presupposed. Whenever the possessive pronoun is stated, the Κύριε is appended with something else, such as, Κύριε ὁ Θεὸς ἡμῶν, Κύριε ἡμῶν Ἰησοῦ Χριστέ.

In the English, though, the vocative is often preceded by a possessive pronoun, unless the archaic *O* is preserved. At any rate, the meaning of *O Lord,* is clearly *our Lord.* This we attempted to bring out by substituting the exclamation O with our. After all, we call God not someone else's God but our own.

23. Ἀχώριστον, primarily means, inseparable, a meaning we have retained here. But indivisible says the same thing although the Greeks in their relentless scrutinizing of terms provide ἀδιαίρετον for indivisible, and some theologians strongly argue on the differences between terms such as, undivided, indivisible, inseparable.

24. Στῶμεν καλῶς, στῶμεν μετὰ φόβου. The καλῶς here obviously means, with the proper attitude inside and the proper posture outside; reverently sums it up well though not as impressively as a freer translation would do. Φόβος, in relation to liturgical admonitions means awe more than fear. Even φόβος Θεοῦ, is doubtful whether it is intended to stress more the punitive power of God than the boundless sense of absolute dependence that a truly religious individual feels and which can only imperfectly be expressed as φόβος, fear.

25. Ἔλεον εἰρήνης, θυσίαν αἰνέσεως, refers to the nature of the Holy Offering. The response says, the Holy Offering is a merciful offering of peace between man and God, for by the Sacrifice on the Cross God provided man with a gratis redemption that would bring peace between Creator and creature. Also, it is a sacrifice of praise on the part of the Lord who by

89

His death offered God the Father the supreme worship of praise. (See detailed discussion of this point in Part II, p. 304).

26. Ἄνω σχῶμεν τὰς καρδίας–ἔχομεν πρὸς τὸν Κύριον, is self-understood in the Greek. In the English, the, *we have, unto the Lord,* is elliptical. It could be supplemented with a poetical verse affirmative of the call of the celebrant to lift up our hearts.

27. Some translators have *angelic hosts* for *Sabaoth.* We have retained the transliterated Hebrew for effect, and further down we alternate between *Hosana* and *Praise the Lord,* thus interpreting the former and keeping a kind of variety that seems to improve the translation of the hymn.

28. παρεδίδοτο, means, *he was being delivered by betrayal.*

29. Τὰ Σὰ ἐκ τῶν Σῶν... This is the act of the Offering on the part of the priest before the invocation of the Holy Spirit to change the visible elements of bread and wine into the Body and Blood of Christ. And these are, undoubtedly, the two most difficult verses in the Liturgy to translate. If they are translated word by word, they make no sense, or, if they do — as with some translations — it is mostly the wrong sense. Two translations from which subsequent translators have copied extensively, are the following:

a. *Thine own of Thine own we offer to Thee,*

90

in all and for all. Even if you are a theologian, the *in all and for all,* require clarification. If you are not a theologian you understand nothing.

b. *Thine own of Thine own we offer to Thee, in behalf of all and for all.* This is wrong in the second verse, because κατὰ πάντα can hardly mean, *in behalf of all.*

The meaning of the Offering is this: we offer to You these Gifts — the sacrificial bread and wine — which are the fruits of Your own creation. And we offer these Gifts κατὰ πάντα, with all, that is, with complete devotion and a grateful heart, without reservations, with our whole existence: καὶ διὰ πάντα, and for all, that is, in return for all the goodness and benefactions You have graciously extended to us. The difficulty lies in the fact that in Greek we use possessive pronouns by themselves and we can put prepositions to work for us as effectively as in no other language, save Latin to a certain extent. This highly condensed type of poetry can hardly sound the same, or even close enough, in any other language.

30. Τὴν λογικήν... λατρείαν. Λογικήν, can hardly mean *reasonable.* The poet calls the bloodless sacrifice in the Liturgy λογικὴ in distinction to an actual sacrificial act, as was the custom with both pagans and Hebrews.

Thus, λογικὴ λατρεία means a sacrificial worship of the intellect, but because the term *intellect* in this context does not express a religious attitude, *spiritual* will do well. . . . *this spiritual and bloodless sacrificial worship*, would amply convey the meaning of the original.

31. . . .εἰς βασιλείας οὐρανῶν πλήρωμα, is translated with, *for the fulfillment of the heavenly kingdom.* The meaning behind it is, *for the heavenly kingdom to be realized in us.* Thus, the kingdom of heaven would be fulfilled as a result of our receiving of the Body and Blood of Christ and, in a way, will be earned by us through Holy Communion.

32. Ἐν πίστει τετελειωμένου, is translated, *made perfect in the faith,* that is, perfected as a result of one's living and productive faith in Christ the Savior. Another interpretation takes ἐν πίστει τετελειωμένου to mean, *having died in faith,* that is, believing in Christ.

33. Ἐν πρώτοις, may be taken to mean, *among the first,* or, *above all.* The intention here is, *First of all,* which is not exactly, *among the first.* Ἐν πρώτοις, is used adverbially in later Greek and simply means, *first,* in distinction to ἐκ δευτέρου, *second.*

34. Εἰς πειρασμόν, has been traditionally translated with *into temptation,* and will certainly be difficult to convince people that Πειρασμὸς in this case means *the test* to which we are

92

subjected in life by God's permission. This test may be in the nature of the pleasures of the flesh as well as the sicknesses of the moral constitution of man, such as glory, power seeking, greediness, accumulation of wealth, lack of compassion, and many others that plague man. Or, it may be in the nature of trials and tribulations, deprivations, ill health, and many other ways in which one's moral fiber is shown and its strength and durability are put to the test. In modern Greek, Πειρασμός also signifies the devil to whom the luring to evil-doing by way of personal pleasures of material origin is attributed. The translation of the Lord's Prayer recently published by a joint Protestant and Catholic commission, also has for εἰς πειρασμὸν *to the test*.

35. ἀπὸ τοῦ πονηροῦ, has been traditionally translated, *from evil*. After much thought and examination of relevant Patristic usage, we have concluded that the reference here is not to evil in abstract or as a force in the world, but to a personification of evil expressed in later Greek with a masculine proper noun, Πειρασμός, the evil One. Thus, even at the risk of ignoring tradition, we have entered *the evil One*, in the sense of St. Matthew's Beelzebul (St. Matthew 10:25), instead of evil as a state of affairs in the field of interrelationships. The above joint Protestant and Catholic commission have also decided to en-

ter *evil one* as a person, thus breaking away from a long standing liturgical tradition and even interfering with the famous music of the Lord's Prayer.

36. Αὐτὸς Δέσποτα... is difficult to translate by trying to follow the order of the emphasis as it is placed in the Greek. The meaning is, *You have done this, You have done that, You have done all these things . . . do also now do this that we ask of You.* The rendering of αὐτὸς by Thou Thyself may be correct in meaning but it can hardly read meaningfully in English. The insertion of an *also* will point out to the fact that He who has done all those things in the past is now asked to do *also* this particular favor for us. This Greek rhetoric apostrophe abounds in the important prayer by which the baptismal water in the sacrament of baptism is sanctified. It has kept in agony many a translator. The *now*, though missing in this particular case, is found in the other prayers containing the apostrophe, and must be understood here, else the causal continuity of the Greek text is broken.

37. Here we have the hierarchical order of receiving Holy Communion: bishops and priests receive Communion by their own hands, but in terms of spiritual reality, by the hand of God. They, in turn, impart Communion to the laity. Clergymen of all three ranks can impart Communion, but only priests and bishops can

make the Epiclesis (the Invocation of the Holy Spirit) and effect the Consecration of the Holy Gifts.

38. Τὰ ἅγια τοῖς ἁγίοις..., the Holy Gifts for the holy people of God. The ἅγιοι here are not the saints in the contemporary meaning of the term. The Greek for saint and holy is the same, hence the misunderstanding. Ἅγιοι, sanctified, are called all those who have been hallowed by their faith in Christ and by receiving His Sacrament. These are the faithful who make up the people of God.

39. ἀξίως, means, in a worthy, deserving manner. Hence, appropriately, befitting a particular situation. In this case, the thanks for which the celebrant is calling, must be commensurate with the situation, that is, with having received the Body and Blood of Christ. But the deserving manner of ἀξιως may be taken to also refer to Christ, that is, these deserving thanks are His due thanks. Primarily, though, ἀξίως means worthily as far as we are concerned, that is, in distinction to ἀναξίως, — unworthily — on our part.

40. πλήρωμα, obviously means the whole body of the Church universal, not only the membership of our particular local church. The word πλήρωμα is primarily applicable to complement-crew of a ship-ark by which the Church of Christ was symbolically pictured.

So, the πλήρωμα of the Church-ship must be the whole complement of the one Church-ark of Christ.

41. The last prayer of all Orthodox ceremonies is called in Greek ’Απόλυσις, dismissal. In Greek, ’Απόλυσις has aquired a traditional sanctity that has completely obliterated the usual sense of *letting someone go, of dismissing him.* And though the priest does ask the people to *depart in peace,* the English *dismissal* does not sound as churchly as the Greek ’Απόλυσις. The almost equivalent Western prayer is called Benediction — final blessing — and apart from an ill-founded fear of our liturgical articulation being confused with Catholic practices, there is nothing to prevent us from calling our Dismissal, Benediction.

42. ’Αντίδωρον, — the blessed bread instead of the Holy Gifts — was originally given only to those who for justifiable reasons were unable to partake of the Holy Gifts, that is, to receive Holy Communion. Today, when for many and just as unjustifiable reasons few receive Communion at every Liturgy, the *antidoron* is distributed to all who have attended the Liturgy. Thus, the *antidoron* has become a tangible symbol of participation in the Liturgy; actually, it is the only personal experience of participation, as the laity have been gradually deprived of singing their responses

to the priest's affirmations of faith, and have been reduced to the role of passive spectators. The Church should reintroduce the participation of the people in the Liturgy, and stringent requirements for Communion — other than the all-important spiritual preparedness — should be adopted to contemporary conditions so as to prove not a hindrance to Communion but the prompting and preparation they ought to be.

OUR BIBLICAL READINGS

(Explanation for worshippers)

The cycle of our Orthodox Biblical Readings (Apostolic and Gospel readings) begins with Easter Sunday. And since Easter is not celebrated on the same day and month each year, no calendar dates can be ascribed to these readings.

The worshipper should follow their sequence beginning with Easter Sunday and may enter his own notations as to calendar dates. It should be noted that the numbering of Sundays begins with the Sunday of All Saints. Sundays between Easter and this Sunday bear their own specific names. Also, from Sunday after Epiphany to the Sunday of the Publican and the Pharisee (the beginning of the Triodion), we have entered no readings because their number varies according to whether Easter falls early or late on a particular year. Interested worshippers should ask their priest early in January to supply them with a list of the unquoted readings.

At the end of the Sunday Biblical Readings, the Apostolic and Gospel passages of the most important feast-days of the Orthodox year are cited.

EASTER SUNDAY

The Apostolic Reading
Acts 1:1-8

In the first book, O Theophilus, I have dealt with all that Jesus began to do and teach, until the day when he was taken up, after he had given commandment through the Holy Spirit to the apostles whom he had chosen. To them he presented himself alive after his passion by many proofs, appearing to them during forty days, and speaking of the kingdom of God. And while staying with them he charged them not to depart from Jerusalem, but to wait for the promise of the Father, which, he said, "you heard from me, for John baptized with water, but before many days you shall be baptized with the Holy Spirit."

So when they had come together, they asked him, "Lord, will you at this time restore the kingdom to Israel?" He said to them, "It is not for you to know times or seasons which the Father has fixed by his own authority. But you shall receive power when the Holy Spirit has come upon you; and you shall be my witnesses in Jerusalem and in all Judea and Samar'ia and to the end of the earth."

The Gospel Reading
St. John 1:1-17

In the beginning was the Word, and the Word was with God, and the Word was God. He was in the beginning with God; all things were made through him, and without him was not anything made that was made. In him was life, and the life was the light of men. The light shines in the darkness, and the darkness has not overcome it.

There was a man sent from God, whose name was John. He came for testimony, to bear witness to the light, that all might believe through him. He was not the light, but came to bear witness to the light.

The true light that enlightens every man was coming into the world. He was in the world, and the world was made through him, yet the world knew him not. He came to his own home, and his own people received him not. But to all who received him, who believed in him name, he gave power to become children of God; who were born, not of blood nor of the will of the flesh nor of the will of man, but of God.

And the Word became flesh and dwelt among us, full of grace and truth; we have beheld his glory, glory as of the only Son from the Father. (John bore witness to him, and cried, "This was he of whom I said, 'He who comes after me ranks before me, for he was before me.'") And from his fulness have we all received, grace upon grace. For the law was given through Moses; grace and truth came through Jesus Christ.

SUNDAY OF ST. THOMAS
The Apostolic Reading
Acts 5:12-20

Now many signs and wonders were done among the people by the hands of the apostles. And they were all together in Solomon's Portico. None of the rest dared join them, but the people held them in high honor. And more than ever believers were added to the Lord, multitudes both of men and women, so that they even carried

100

out the sick into the streets, and laid them on beds and pallets, that as Peter came by at least his shadow might fall on some of them. The people also gathered from the towns around Jerusalem, bringing the sick and those afflicted with unclean spirits, and they were all healed.

But the high priest rose up and all who were with him, that is, the party of the Sad'ducees, and filled with jealousy they arrested the apostles and put them in the common prison. But at night an angel of the Lord opened the prison doors and brought them out and said, "Go and stand in the temple and speak to the people all the words of this Life."

The Gospel Reading
St. John 20:19-31

On the evening of that day, the first day of the week, the doors being shut where the disciples were, for fear of the Jews, Jesus came and stood among them and said to them, "Peace be with you." When he had said this, he showed them his hands and his side. Then the disciples were glad when they saw the Lord. Jesus said to them again, "Peace be with you. As the Father has sent me, even so I send you." And when he had said this, he breathed on them, and said to them, "Receive the Holy Spirit. If you forgive the sins of any, they are forgiven; if you retain the sins of any, they are retained."

Now Thomas, one of the twelve, called the Twin, was not with them when Jesus came. So the other disciples told him, "We have seen the Lord." But he said to them, "Unless I see in his hands the print of the nails, and place my finger in the mark of the nails,

101

and place my hand in his side, I will not believe."

Eight days later, his disciples were again in the house, and Thomas was with them. The doors were shut, but Jesus came and stood among them, and said, "Peace be with you." Then he said to Thomas, "Put your finger here, and see my hands; and put out your hand, and place it in my side; do not be faithless, but believing." Thomas answered him, "My Lord and my God!" Jesus said to him, "Have you believed because you have seen me? Blessed are those who have not seen and yet believe."

Now Jesus did many other signs in the presence of the disciples, which are not written in this book; but these are written that you may believe that Jesus is the Christ, the Son of God, and that believing you may have life in his name.

SUNDAY OF THE MYRRH-BEARERS

The Apostolic Reading
Acts 6:1-7

Now in these days when the disciples were increasing in number, the Hellenists murmured against the Hebrews because their widows were neglected in the daily distribution. And the twelve summoned the body of the disciples and said, "It is not right that we should give up preaching the word of God to serve tables. Therefore, brethren, pick out from among you seven men of good repute, full of the Spirit and of wisdom, whom we may appoint to this duty. But we will devote ourselves to prayer and to the ministry of the word." And what they said pleased the whole multitude, and they chose Stephen, a man full of faith and of the

Holy Spirit, and Philip, and Proch'orus, and Nica'nor, and Timon, and Par'menas, and Nicola'us, a proselyte of Antioch. These they set before the apostles, and they prayed and laid their hands upon them.

The Gospel Reading
St. Mark 15, 43-47, 16, 1-8

At that time, Joseph of Arimathea, a respected member of the council, who was also himself looking for the kingdom of God, took courage and went to Pilate, and asked for the body of Jesus. And Pilate wondered if he were already dead; and summoning the centurion, he asked him whether he was already dead. And when he learned from the centurion that he was dead, he granted the body to Joseph. And he bought a linen shroud, and taking him down, wrapped him in the linen shroud, and laid him in a tomb which had been hewn out of the rock; and he rolled a stone against the door of the tomb. Mary Magdalene and Mary the mother of Joses saw where he was laid.

And when the sabbath was past, Mary Magdalene, and Mary the mother of James, and Salome, bought spices, so that they might go and anoint him. And very early on the first day of the week they went to the tomb when the sun had risen. And they were saying to one another, "Who will roll away the stone for us from the door of the tomb?" And looking up, they saw that the stone was rolled back; for it was very large. And entering the tomb, they saw a young man sitting on the right side, dressed in a white robe; and they were amazed. And he said to them, "Do not be amazed; you seek Jesus of Nazareth, who was crucified. He has risen, he is not here; see the place where they laid him. But go, tell his disciples and Peter that he is going before you to Galilee; there you will see him, as he told you." And they went out and fled from the tomb; for trembling and astonishment had come upon them; and they said nothing to any one, for they were afraid.

SUNDAY OF THE PARALYTIC
The Apostolic Reading
Acts 9:32-42

Now as Peter went here and there among them all, he came down also to the saints that lived at Lydda. There he found a man named Aene'as, who had been bedridden for eight years and was paralyzed. And Peter said to him, "Aene'as, Jesus Christ heals you; rise and make your bed." And immediately he rose. And all the residents of Lydda and Sharon saw him, and they turned to the Lord.

Now there was at Joppa a disciple named Tabitha, which means Dorcas. She was full of good works and acts of charity. In those days she fell sick and died; and when they had washed her, they laid her in an upper room. Since Lydda was near Joppa, the disciples, hearing that Peter was there, sent two men to him entreating him, "Please come to us without delay." So Peter rose and went with them. And when he had come, they took him to the upper room. All the widows stood beside him weeping, and showing tunics and other garments which Dorcas made while she was with them. But Peter put them all outside and knelt down and prayed; then turning to the body he said, "Tabitha, rise." And she opened her eyes, and when she saw Peter she sat up. And he gave her his hand and lifted her up. Then calling the saints and widows

he presented her alive. And it became known throughout all Joppa, and many believed in the Lord.

The Gospel Reading
St. John 5, 1-15

At that time, Jesus went up to Jerusalem. Now there
is in Jerusalem by the Sheep Gate a pool, in Hebrew
called Bethesda which has five porticoes. In these lay a
multitude of invalids, blind, lame, paralyzed, waiting
for the moving of the water; for an angel of the Lord
went down at certain seasons into the pool, and
troubled the water; whoever stepped in first after the
troubling of the water was healed of whatever disease
he had. One man was there, who had been ill for thirty-
eight years. When Jesus saw him and knew that he
had been lying there a long time, he said to him, "Do
you want to be healed?" The sick man answered him,
"Sir, I have no man to put me into the pool when the
water is troubled, and while I am going another steps
down before me." Jesus said to him, "Rise, take up
your pallet, and walk." And at once the man was
healed, and he took up his pallet and walked.

Now that day was the sabbath. So the Jews said to
the man who was cured, "It is the sabbath, it is not
lawful for you to carry your pallet." But he answered
them. "The man who healed me said to me, " 'Take up
your pallet, and walk.' " They asked him, "Who is the
man who said to you, 'Take up your pallet, and walk'?"
Now the man who had been healed did not know who
it was, for Jesus had withdrawn, as there was a crowd
in the place. Afterward, Jesus found him in the temple,
and said to him, "See, you are well! Sin no more, that
nothing worse befall you." The man went away and
told the Jews that it was Jesus who had healed him.

SUNDAY OF THE SAMARITAN WOMAN

The Apostolic Reading
Acts 11:19-30

Now those who were scattered because of the persecution that arose over Stephen traveled as far as Phoenicia and Cyprus and Antioch, speaking the word to none except Jews. But there were some of them, men of Cyprus and Cyre'ne, who on coming to Antioch spoke to the Greeks also, preaching the Lord Jesus. And the hand of the Lord was with them, and a great number that believed turned to the Lord. News of this came to the ears of the church in Jerusalem, and they sent Barnabas to Antioch. When he came and saw the grace of God, he was glad; and he exhorted them all to remain faithful to the Lord with steadfast purpose; for he was a good man, full of the Holy Spirit and of faith. And a large company was added to the Lord. So Barnabas went to Tarsus to look for Saul; and when he had found him, he brought him to Antioch. For a whole year they met with the church, and taught a large company of people; and in Antioch the disciples were for the first time called Christians.

Now in these days prophets came down from Jerusalem to Antioch. And one of them named Ag'abus stood up and foretold by the Spirit that there would be a great famine over all the world; and this took place in the days of Claudius. And the disciples determined, every one according to his ability, to send relief to the brethren who lived in Judea; and they did so, sending it to the elders by the hand of Barnabas and Saul.

The Gospel Reading
St. John 4:5-42

At that time Jesus came to a city of Samaria, called Sychar, near the field that Jacob gave to his son Joseph. Jacob's well was there, and so Jesus, wearied as he was with his journey, sat down beside the well. It was about the sixth hour.

There came a woman of Samaria to draw water. Jesus said to her, "Give me a drink." For his disciples had gone away into the city to buy food. The Samaritan woman said to him, "How is it that you, a Jew, ask a drink of me, a woman of Samaria?" For Jews have no dealings with Samaritans. Jesus answered her, "If you knew the gift of God, and who it is that is saying to you, 'Give me a drink,' you would have asked him and he would have given you living water." The woman said to him, "Sir, you have nothing to draw with, and the well is deep; where do you get that living water? Are you greater than our father Jacob, who gave us the well, and drank from it himself, and his sons, and his cattle?" Jesus said to her, "Every one who drinks of this water will thirst again, but whoever drinks of the water that I shall give him will never thirst; the water that I shall give him will become in him a spring of water welling up to eternal life." The woman said to him, "Sir, give me this water, that I may not thirst, nor come here to draw."

Jesus said to her, "Go, call your husband, and come here." The woman answered him, "I have no husband." Jesus said to her, "You are right in saying, 'I have no husband'; for you have had five husbands, and he whom you now have is not your husband; this you said truly." The woman said to him, "Sir, I perceive that you are a prophet. Our fathers worshiped on this mountain; and you say that in Jerusalem is the place where men ought to worship." Jesus said to her, "Woman, believe me, the hour is coming when neither on this mountain nor in Jerusalem will you worship the Father. You worship what you do not know; we worship what we know, for salvation is from the Jews. But the hour is coming, and now is, when the true worshipers will worship the Father in spirit and truth, for such the Father seeks to worship him. God is spirit, and those who worship him must worship in spirit and truth." The woman said to him, "I know that Messiah is coming (he who is called Christ); when he comes, he will show us all things." Jesus said to her, "I who speak to you am he."

Just then his disciples came. They marveled that he was talking with a woman, but none said, "What do you wish?" or, "Why are you talking with her?" So the woman left her water jar, and went away into the city, and said to the people, "Come, see a man who told me all that I ever did. Can this be the Christ?" They went out of the city and were coming to him.

Meanwhile the disciples besought him, saying, "Rabbi, eat." But he said to them, "I have food to eat of which you do not know." So the disciples said to one another, "Has any one brought him food?" Jesus said to them, "My food is to do the will of him who sent me, and to accomplish his work. Do you not say, 'There are yet four months, then comes the harvest'? I tell you, lift up your eyes, and see how the fields are already white for harvest. He who reaps receives wages, and gathers fruit for eternal life, so that sower and reaper may rejoice together. For here the saying holds, true, 'One sows and another reaps.' I sent you to reap that for which you did not labor; others have labored, and you have entered into their labor."

Many Samaritans from that city believed in him because of the woman's testimony, "He told me all that I ever did." So when the Samaritans came to him, they asked him to stay with them; and he stayed there two days. And many more believed because of his word. They said to the woman, "It is no longer because of your words that we believe, for we have heard for ourselves, and we know that this is indeed Christ the Savior of the world."

SUNDAY OF THE BLIND MAN

The Apostolic Reading
Acts 16:16-34

As we were going to the place of prayer, we were met by a slave girl who had a spirit of divination and brought her owners much gain by soothsaying. She followed Paul and us, crying, "These men are servants of the Most High God, who proclaim to you the way of salvation. And this she did for many days. But Paul was annoyed, and turned and said to the spirit, "I charge you in the name of Jesus Christ to come out of her." And it came out that very hour.

But when her owners saw that their hope of gain was gone, they seized Paul and Silas and dragged them into the market place before the rulers; and when they had brought them to the magistrates they said, "These men are Jews and they are disturbing our city. They advocate customs which it is not lawful for us Romans to accept or practice." The crowd joined in attacking them; and the magistrates tore the garments off them and gave orders to beat them with rods. And when they had inflicted many blows upon them, they threw them into prison, charging the jailer to keep them safely. Having received this charge, he put them into the inner prison and fastened their feet in the stocks.

But about midnight Paul and Silas were praying and singing hymns to God, and the prisoners were listening to them, and suddenly there was a great earthquake, so that the foundations of the prison were shaken; and immediately all the doors were opened and every one's fetters were unfastened. When the jailer woke and saw that the prison doors were open, he drew his sword and was about to kill himself, supposing that the prisoners had escaped. But Paul cried with a loud voice, "Do not harm yourself, for we are all here." And he called for lights and rushed in, and trembling with fear he fell down before Paul and Silas, and brought them out and said, "Men, what must I do to be saved?" And they said, "Believe in the Lord Jesus, and you will be saved, you and your household." And they spoke the word of the Lord to him and to all that were in his house. And he took them the same hour of the night, and washed their wounds, and he was baptized at once, with all his family. Then he brought them up into his house, and set food before them; and he rejoiced with all his household that he had believed in God.

The Gospel Reading
St. John 9:1-38

At that time, as Jesus passed by, he saw a man blind from his birth. And his disciples asked him, "Rabbi, who sinned, this man or his parents, that he was born blind?" Jesus answered, "It was not that this man sinned, or his parents, but that the works of God might be made manifest in him. We must work the works of him who sent me, while it is day; night comes, when no one can work. As long as I am in the world, I am the light of the world." As he said this, he spat on the ground and made clay of the spittle and anointed the man's eyes with the clay, saying to him, "Go, wash in the pool of Siloam" (which means Sent). So he went and washed and came back seeing. The neighbors and those who had seen him before as a beggar, said, "Is not this the man who used to sit and beg?" Some said, "It is he;" others said, "No, but he is like him." He said, "I am the man." They said to him, "Then how were your eyes opened?" He answered, "The man called Jesus made clay and anointed my eyes and said to me, 'Go to Siloam and wash'; so I went and washed and received my sight." They said to him, "Where is he?" He said, "I do not know."

They brought to the Pharisees the man who had formerly been blind. Now it was a sabbath day when Jesus made the clay and opened his eyes. The Pharisees again asked him how he had received his sight. And he said to them, "He put clay on my eyes and I washed, and I see." Some of the Pharisees said, "This man is not from God, for he does not keep the sabbath." But others said, "How can a man who is a sinner do such signs?" There was a division among them. So they again said to the blind man, "What do you say about him, since he has opened your eyes?" He said, "He is a prophet."

The Jews did not believe that he had been blind and had received his sight, until they called the parents of the man who had received his sight, and asked them, "Is this your son, who you say was born blind? How then does he now see?" His parents answered, "We know that this is our son, and that he was born blind; but how he now sees we do not know, nor do we know who opened his eyes. Ask him; he is of age, he will speak for himself." His parents said this because they feared the Jews, for the Jews had already agreed that if any one should confess him to be Christ, he was to be put out of the synagogue. Therefore his parents said, "He is of age, ask him."

So for the second time they called the man who had been blind, and said to him, "Give God the praise; we know that this man is a sinner." He answered, "Whether he is a sinner, I do not know; one thing I know, that though I was blind, now I see." They said to him, "What did he do to you? How did he open eyes?" He answered them, "I have told you already, and you would not listen. Why do you want to hear it again? Do you too want to become his disciples?" And they reviled him, saying, "You are his disciple, but we are disciples of Moses. We know that God has spoken to Moses, but as for this man, we do not know where he comes from." The man answered, "Why, this is a marvel! You do not know where he comes from, and yet he opened my eyes. We know that God does not listen to sinners, but if any one is a worshiper of God and does his will, God listens to him. Never since the world began has it been heard that any one opened the eyes of a man born blind. If this man were not from God, he could do nothing." They answered him, "You were born in utter sin, and would you teach us?" And they cast him out.

Jesus heard that they had cast him out, and having

found him he said, "Do you believe in the Son of man?"
He answered, "And who is he, sir, that I may believe
in him?" Jesus said to him, "You have seen him, and
it is he who speaks to you." He said, "Lord, I believe";
and he worshiped him.

SUNDAY OF THE HOLY FATHERS

The Apostolic Reading
Acts 20:16-18; 28-36

Paul had decided to sail past Ephesus, so that he
might not have to spend time in Asia; for he was has-
tening to be in Jerusalem, if possible, on the day of
Pentecost. And from Miletus he sent to Ephesus and
called to him the elders of the church. And when they
came to him, he said to them: Take heed to yourselves
and to all the flock, in which the Holy Spirit has made
you guardians, to feed the church of the Lord which
he obtained with his own blood. I know that after my
departure fierce wolves will come in among you, not
sparing the flock; and from among your own selves
will arise men speaking perverse things, to draw away
the disciples after them. Therefore be alert, remembering that for three years I did not cease night or day to
admonish every one with tears. And now I commend
you to God and to the word of his grace, which is able
to build you up and to give you the inheritance among
all those who are sanctified. I coveted no one's silver
or gold or apparel. You yourselves know that these
hands ministered to my necessities, and to those who
were with me. In all things I have shown you that by
so toiling one must help the weak, remembering the
words of the Lord Jesus, how he said, "It is more

blessed *to give than to receive"*. And when he had spoken thus, he knelt down and prayed with them all.

The Gospel Reading
St. John 17:1-13

At that time, Jesus lifted up his eyes to heaven and said, "Father, the hour has come; glorify thy Son that the Son may glorify Thee, since Thou hast given him power over all flesh, to give eternal life to all whom Thou hast given him. And this is eternal life, that they know Thee the only true God, and Jesus Christ whom Thou hast sent. I glorified Thee on earth, having accomplished the work which Thou gavest me to do; and now, Father glorify Thou me in Thy own presence with the glory which I had with Thee before the world was made.

"I have manifested Thy name to the men whom Thou gavest me out of the world; thine they were, and Thou gavest them to me, and they have kept Thy word. Now they know that everything that Thou hast given me is from Thee; for I have given them the words which Thou gavest me, and they have received them and know in truth that I came from Thee; and they have believed that Thou didst send me. I am praying for them; I am not praying for the world but for those whom Thou hast given me, for they are Thine; all mine are Thine, and Thine are mine, and I am glorified in them. And now I am no more in the world, but they are in the world, and I am coming to Thee. Holy Father, keep them in Thy name, which Thou hast given me, that they may be one, even as we are one. While I was with them, I kept them in Thy name, which Thou hast given me; I have guarded them, and none of them is lost but the son of perdition, that the scripture might *be fulfilled. But now I am coming to Thee; and these things I speak in the world, that they may have my joy fulfilled in themselves.*

THE PENTECOST

The Apostolic Reading
Acts 2:1-11

When the day of Pentecost had come, they were all together in one place. And suddenly a sound came from heaven like the rush of a mighty wind, and it filled all the house where they were sitting. And there appeared to them tongues as of fire, distributed and resting on each one of them. And they were all filled with the Holy Spirit and began to speak in other tongues, as the Spirit gave them utterance.

Now there were dwelling in Jerusalem Jews, devout men from every nation under heaven. And at this sound the multitude came together, and they were bewildered, because each one heard them speaking in his own language. And they were amazed and wondered, saying, "Are not all these who are speaking Galileans? And how is it that we hear, each of us in his own native language? Par'thians and Medes and Elamites and residents of Mesopota'mia, Judea and Cappado'cia, Pontus and Asia, Phryg'ia and Pamphyl'ia, Egypt and the parts of Libya belonging to Cyre'ne, and visitors from Rome, both Jews and proselytes, Cretans and Arabians, we hear them telling in our own tongues the mighty works of God."

The Gospel Reading
St. John 7:37-52

On the last day of the feast, the great day, Jesus stood up and proclaimed, "If any one thirst, let him come to me and drink. He who believes in me, as the scripture has said, 'Out of his heart shall flow rivers of living water." Now this he said about the Spirit, which those who believed in him were to receive; for as yet the Spirit had not been given, because Jesus was not yet glorified.

When they heard these words, some of the people said, "This is really the prophet." Others said, "This is the Christ." But some said, "Is the Christ to come from Galilee? Has not the scripture said that the Christ is descended from David, and comes from Bethlehem, the village where David was? So there was a division among the people over him. Some of them wanted to arrest him, but no one laid hands on him.

The officers then went back to the chief priests and Pharisees, who said to them, "Why did you not bring him?" The officers answered, "No man ever spoke like this man!" The Pharisees answered them, "Are you led astray, you also? Have any of the authorities or of the Pharisees believed in him? But this crowd, who do not know the law, are accursed." Nicodemus, who had gone to him before, and who was one of them, said to them, "Does our law judge a man without first giving him a hearing and learning what he does?" They replied, "Are you from Galilee too? Search and you will see that no prophet is to rise from Galilee."

Again Jesus spoke to them, saying, "I am the light of the world; he who follows me will not walk in darkness, but will have the light of life."

FIRST SUNDAY
SUNDAY OF ALL SAINTS

The Apostolic Reading
Hebrews 11:33-40

Brethren, the saints through faith conquered kingdoms, enforced justice, received promises, stopped the
mouths of lions, quenched raging fire, escaped the edge
of the sword, won strength out of weakness, became
mighty in war, put foreign armies to flight. Women
received their dead by resurrection. Some were tortured, refusing to accept release, that they might rise
again to a better life. Others suffered mocking and
scourging, and even chains and imprisonment. They
were stoned, they were sawn in two, they were killed
with the sword; they went about in skins of sheep and
goats, destitute, afflicted, ill-treated (of whom the
world was not worthy) wandering over deserts and
mountains, and in dens and caves of the earth. And all
these, though well attested by their faith, did not receive what was promised, since God had foreseen
something better for us, that apart from us they should
not be made perfect.

The Gospel Reading
St. Matthew 10:32-33, 37-38, 19-27-30

The Lord said to His disciples: Every one who ac-
knowledges me before men, I also will acknowledge
him before my Father who is in heaven; but whoever
denies me before men, I also will deny him before my
Father who is in heaven.

He who loves father or mother more than me is not worthy of me; and he who loves son or daughter more than me is not worthy of me; and he who does not take his cross and follow me is not worthy of me. Then Peter said in reply, "Lo, we have left everything and followed you. What then shall we have?" Jesus said to them, "Truly, I say to you, in the new world, when the Son of man shall sit on his glorious throne, you who have followed me will also sit on twelve thrones, judging the twelve tribes of Israel. And every one who has left houses or brothers or sisters or father or mother or children or lands, for my name's sake, will receive a hundredfold, and inherit eternal life. But many that are first will be last, and the last first.

SECOND SUNDAY
The Apostolic Reading
Romans 2:10-16

Brethren, glory and honor and peace for every one who does good, the Jew first and also the Greek. For God shows no partiality.

All who have sinned without the law will also perish without the law, and all who have sinned under the law will be judged by the law. For it is not the hearers of the law who are righteous before God, but the doers of the law who will be justified. When Gentiles who have not the law do by nature what the law requires, they are a law to themselves, even though they do not have the law. They show that what the law requires is written on their hearts, while their conscience also bears witness and their conflicting thoughts accuse or perhaps excuse them on that day when, according to

118

my gospel, God judges the secrets of men by Christ
Jesus.

The Gospel Reading
St. Matthew 4:18-23

At that time, Jesus walked by the Sea of Galilee,
he saw two brothers, Simon who is called Peter and
Andrew his brother, casting a net into the sea; for they
were fishermen. And he said to them, "Follow me, and
I will make you fishers of men." Immediately they left
their nets and followed him. And going on from there he
saw two other brothers, James the son of Zebedee and
John his brother, in the boat with Zebedee their father,
mending their nets, and he called them. Immediately
they left the boat and their father, and followed him.

And he went about all Galilee, teaching in their
synagogues and preaching the gospel of the kingdom
and healing every disease and every infirmity among
the people.

THIRD SUNDAY

The Apostolic Reading
Romans 5:1-10

Therefore, since we are justified by faith, we have
peace with God through our Lord Jesus Christ. Through
him we have obtained access to this grace in which we
stand, and we rejoice in our hope of sharing the glory
of God. More than that, we rejoice in our sufferings,
knowing that suffering produces endurance, and endurance produces character, and character produces hope,
and hope does not disappoint us, because God's love

has been poured into our hearts through the Holy Spirit which has been given to us.

While we were still weak, at the right time Christ died for the ungodly. Why, one will hardly die for a righteous man — though perhaps for a good man one will dare even to die. But God shows his love for us in that while we were yet sinners Christ died for us. Since, therefore, we are now justified by his blood, much more shall we be saved by him from the wrath of God. For if while we were enemies we were reconciled to God by the death of his Son, much more, now that we are reconciled, shall we be saved by his life.

The Gospel Reading
St. Matthew 6:22-33

The Lord said: "The eye is the lamp of the body. So, if your eye is sound, your whole body will be full of light; but if your eye is not sound, your whole body will be full of darkness. If then the light in you is darkness, how great is the darkness!

"No one can serve two masters; for either he will hate the one and love the other, or he will be devoted to the one and despise the other. You cannot serve God and mammon.

"Therefore I tell you, do not be anxious about your life, what you shall eat or what you shall drink, nor about your body, what you shall put on. Is not life more than food, and the body more than clothing? Look at the birds of the air: they neither sow nor reap nor gather into barns, and yet your heavenly Father feeds them. Are you not of more value than they? And which of you by being anxious can add one cubit to his span of life? And why are you anxious about clothing? Consider the lilies of the field, how they grow; they neither toil nor spin; yet I tell you, even Solomon in all his glory was not arrayed like one of these. But if God so clothes the grass of the field, which today is alive and tomorrow is thrown into the oven, will he not much more clothe you, O men of little faith? Therefore do not be anxious, saying, 'What shall we eat?' or 'What shall we drink?' or 'What shall we wear?' For the Gentiles seek all these things; and your heavenly Father knows that you need them all. But seek first his kingdom and his righteousness, and all these things shall be yours as well.

FOURTH SUNDAY

The Apostolic Reading
Romans 6:18-23

Brethren, having been set free from sin, have become slaves of righteousness. I am speaking in human terms, because of your natural limitations. For just as you once yielded your members to impurity and to greater and greater iniquity, so now yield your members to righteousness for sanctification.

When you were slaves of sin, you were free in regard to righteousness. But then what return did you get from the things of which you are now ashamed? The end of those things is death. But now that you have been set free from sin and have become slaves of God, the return you get is sanctification and its end, eternal life. For the wages of sin is death, but the free gift of God is eternal life in Christ Jesus our Lord.

The Gospel Reading
St. Matthew 8:5-13

At that time, as Jesus entered Capernaum, a centurion came forward to him, beseeching him and saying, "Lord, my servant is lying paralyzed at home, in terrible distress.' And he said to him, "I will come and heal him." But the centurion answered him, "Lord, I am not worthy to have you come under my roof; but only say the word, and my servant will be healed. For I am a man under authority, with soldiers under me; and I say to one, 'Go,' and he goes, and to another, 'Come," and he comes, and to my slave, 'Do this,' and he does it." When Jesus heard him, he marveled, and said to those who followed him, "Truly, I say to you, not even in Israel have I found such faith. I tell you, many will come from east and west and sit at table with Abraham, Isaac, and Jacob in the kingdom of heaven, while the sons of the kingdom will be thrown into the outer darkness; there men will weep and gnash their teeth." And to the centurion Jesus said, "Go; be it done for you as you have believed." And the servant was healed at that very moment.

FIFTH SUNDAY

The Apostolic Reading
Romans 10:1-10

Brethren, my heart's desire and prayer to God for them is that they may be saved. I bear them witness that they have a zeal for God, but it is not enlightened. For, being ignorant of the righteousness that comes from God and seeking to establish their own, they did not submit to God's righteousness. For Christ is the end of the law, that every one who has faith may be justified.

Moses writes that the man who practices the righteousness which is based on the law shall live by it. But the righteousness based on faith says, Do not say in your heart, "Who will ascend into heaven?" (that is, to bring Christ down) or "Who will descend into the abyss?" (that is, to bring Christ up from the dead). But what does it say? The word is near you, on your lips and in your heart (that is, the word of faith which we preach); because, if you confess with your lips that Jesus is Lord and believe in your heart that God raised him from the dead, you will be saved. For man believes with his heart and so is justified, and he confesses with his lips and so is saved.

The Gospel Reading
St. Matthew 8:28-34, 9:1

At that time, when Jesus came to the other side, to the country of the Gardarenes, two demoniacs met him, coming out of the tombs, so fierce that no one could pass that way. And behold, they cried out, "What have you to do with us, O Son of God? Have you come here to torment us before the time?" Now a herd of many swine was feeding at some distance from them. And the demons begged him, "If you cast us out, send us away into the herd of swine." And he said to them, "Go." So they came out and went into the swine; and behold, the whole herd rushed down the steep bank into the sea, and perished in the waters. The herdsmen fled, and going into the city they told everything, and what had happened to the demoniacs. And behold, all the city came out to meet Jesus; and when they saw him, they begged him to leave their neighborhood.

And getting into a boat he crossed over and came to his own city.

SIXTH SUNDAY

The Apostolic Reading
Romans 12:6-14

Brethren, *having gifts that differ according to the grace given to us, let us use them: if prophecy, in proportion to our faith; if service, in our serving; he who teaches, in his teaching; he who exhorts, in his exhortation; he who contributes, in liberality; he who gives aid, with zeal; he who does acts of mercy, with cheerfulness.*

Let love be genuine; hate what is evil, hold fast to what is good; love one another with brotherly affection; outdo one another in showing honor. Never flag in zeal, be aglow with the spirit, serve the Lord. Rejoice in your hope, be patient in tribulation, be constant in prayer. Contribute to the needs of the saints, practice hospitality.

Bless those who persecute you; bless and do not curse them.

The Gospel Reading
St. Matthew 9:1-8

At that time, *getting into a boat Jesus crossed over and came to his own city. And behold, they brought to him a paralytic, lying on his bed; and when Jesus saw their faith he said to the paralytic, "Take heart, my son; your sins are forgiven." And behold, some of the scribes said to themselves, "This man is blaspheming." But Jesus, knowing their thoughts, said, "Why do you think evil in your hearts? For which is easier, to say,*

'Your sins are forgiven,' or to say, 'Rise and walk'? But that you may know that the Son of man has authority on earth to forgive sins" — he then said to the paralytic — "Rise, take up your bed and go home." And he rose and went home. When the crowds saw it, they were afraid, and they glorified God, who had given such authority to men.

SEVENTH DAY

The Apostolic Reading
Romans 15:1-7

Brethren, we who are strong ought to bear with the failings of the weak, and not to please ourselves; let each of us please his neighbor for his good, to edify him. For Christ did not please himself; but, as it is written, "The reproaches of those who reproached Thee fell on me." For whatever was written in former days was written for our instruction, that by steadfastness and by the encouragement of the scriptures we might have hope. May the God of steadfastness and encouragement grant you to live in such harmony with one another, in accord with Christ Jesus, that together you may with one voice glorify the God and Father of our Lord Jesus Christ.

Welcome one another, therefore, as Christ has welcomed you, for the glory of God.

The Gospel Reading
St. Matthew 9:27-35

At that time, as Jesus passed on from there, two blind men followed him, crying aloud, "Have mercy on us, Son of David." When he entered the house, the blind men came to him; and Jesus said to them, "Do you believe that I am able to do this?" They said to him, "Yes, Lord." Then he touched their eyes, saying, According to your faith be it done to you." And their eyes were opened. And Jesus sternly charged them, "See that no one knows it." But they went away and spread his fame through all that district.

As they were going away, behold, a dumb demoniac was brought to him. And when the demon had been cast out, the dumb man spoke; and the crowds marveled, saying, "Never was anything like this seen in Israel." But the Pharisees said, "He casts out demons by the prince of demons."

And Jesus went about all the cities and villages, teaching in their synagogues and preaching the gospel of the kingdom, and healing every disease and every infirmity among people.

EIGHTH SUNDAY

The Apostolic Reading
Corinthians 1:10-18

Brethren, I appeal to you, brethren, by the name of our Lord Jesus Christ, that all of you agree and that there be no dissensions among you, but that you be united in the same mind and the same judgment. For it has been reported to me by Chlo'e's people that there is quarrelling among you, my brethren. What I mean is that each one of you says, "I belong to Paul," or "I belong to Apol'los," or "I belong to Cephas," or "I belong to Christ." Is Christ divided? Was Paul crucified for you? Or were you baptized in the name of Paul? I am thankful that I baptized none of you except

Crispus and Ga'ius; lest any one should say that you were baptized in my name. (I did baptize also the household of Steph'anas. Beyond that, I do not know whether I baptized any one else.) For Christ did not send me to baptize but to preach the gospel, and not with eloquent wisdom, lest the cross of Christ be emptied of its power.

For the word of the cross is folly to those who are perishing, but to us who are being saved it is the power of God.

The Gospel Reading
St. Matthew 14:14-22

At that time, Jesus saw a great throng; and he had compassion on them, and healed their sick. When it was evening, the disciples came to him and said, "This is a lonely place, and the day is now over; send the crowds away to go into the villages and buy food for themselves." Jesus said, "They need not go away; you give them something to eat." They said to him, "We have only five loaves here and two fish." And he said, "Bring them here to me." Then he ordered the crowds to sit down on the grass; and taking the five loaves and the two fish he looked up to heaven, and blessed, and broke and gave the loaves to the disciples, and the disciples gave them to the crowds. And they all ate and were satisfied. And they took up twelve baskets full of the broken pieces left over. And those who ate were about five thousand men, besides women and children.

Then he made the disciples get into the boat and go before him to the other side, while he dismissed the crowds.

NINTH SUNDAY

The Apostolic Reading
Corinthians 3:9-17

Brethren, we are God's fellow workers; you are God's field, God's building.

According to the grace of God given to me, like a skilled master builder I laid a foundation, and another man is building upon it. Let each man take care how he builds upon it. For no other foundation can any one lay than that which is laid, which is Jesus Christ. Now if any one builds on the foundation with gold, silver, precious stones, wood, hay, straw — each man's work will become manifest; for the Day will disclose it, because it will be revealed with fire, and the fire will test what sort of work each one has done. If the work which any man has built on the foundation survives, he will receive a reward. If any man's work is burned up, he will suffer loss, though he himself will be saved, but only as through fire.

Do you not know that you are God's temple and that God's Spirit dwells in you? If any one destroys God's temple, God will destroy him. For God's temple is holy, and that temple you are.

The Gospel Reading
St. Matthew 14:22-34

At that time, Jesus made the disciples get into the boat and go before him to the other side, while he dismissed the crowds. And after he had dismissed the crowds, he went up into the hills by himself to pray. When evening came, he was there alone, but the boat by this time was many furlongs distant from the land, beaten by the waves; for the wind was against them.

128

And in the fourth watch of the night he came to them, walking on the sea. But when the disciples saw him walking on the sea, they were terrified, saying, "It is a ghost!" And they cried out for fear. But immediately he spoke to them, saying, "Take heart, it is I; have no fear."

And Peter answered him, "Lord, if it is you, bid me come to you on the water.' He said, "Come." So Peter got out of the boat and walked on the water and came to Jesus; but when he saw the wind, he was afraid, and beginning to sink he cried out, "Lord, save me." Jesus immediately reached out his hand and caught him, saying to him, "O man of little faith, why did you doubt?" And when they got into the boat, the wind ceased. And those in the boat worshiped him, saying, "Truly you are the Son of God."

And when they had crossed over, they came to land at Gennesaret.

TENTH SUNDAY

The Apostolic Reading
I Corinthians 4:9-16

For I think that God has exhibited us apostles as last of all, like men sentenced to death; because we have become a spectacle to the world, to angels and to men. We are fools for Christ's sake, but you are wise in Christ. We are weak, but you are strong. You are held in honor, but we in disrepute. To the present hour we hunger and thirst, we are ill-clad and buffeted and homeless, and we labor, working with our own hands. When reviled, we bless; when persecuted, we endure; when slandered, we try to conciliate; we have become, and are now, as the refuse of the world, the offscouring of all things.

I do not write this to make you ashamed, but to admonish you as my beloved children. For though you have countless guides in Christ, you do not have many fathers. For I became your father in Christ Jesus through the gospel. I urge you, then, be imitators of me.

The Gospel Reading
St. Matthew 17:14-23

At that time, a man came up to him and kneeling before him said, "Lord, have mercy on my son, for he is an epileptic and he suffers terribly; for often he falls into the fire, and often into the water. And I brought him to your disciples, and they could not heal him." And Jesus answered, "O faithless and perverse generation, how long am I to be with you? How long am I to bear with you? Bring him here to me." And Jesus rebuked him, and the demon came out of him, and the boy was cured instantly. Then the disciples came to Jesus privately and said. "Why could we not cast it out?" He said to them, "Because of your little faith. For truly, I say to you, if you have faith as a grain of mustard seed, you will say to this mountain, 'Move hence to yonder place,' and it will move; and nothing will be impossible to you."

As they were gathering in Galilee, Jesus said to them, "The Son of man is to be delivered into the hands of men, and they will kill him, and he will be raised on the third day."

ELEVENTH SUNDAY

The Apostolic Reading
I Corinthians 9:2-12

Brethren, *if to others I am not an apostle, at least I am to you; for you are the seal of my apostleship in the Lord. This is my defense to those who would examine me. Do we not have the right to our food and drink? Do we not have the right to be accompanied by a wife, as the other apostles and the brethren of the Lord and Cephas? Or is it only Barnabas and I who have no right to refrain from working for a living? Who serves as a soldier at his own expense? Who plants a vineyard without eating any of its fruit? Who tends a flock without getting some of the milk? Do I say this on human authority? Does not the Lord say the same? For it is written in the law of Moses, "you shall not muzzle an ox when it is treading out the grain". Is it for oxen that God is concerned? Does he not speak entirely for our sake? It was written for our sake, because the plowman should plow in hope and the thresher thresh in hope of a share in the crop. If we have sown spiritual good among you, is it too much if we reap your material benefits? If others share this rightful claim upon you, do not we still more? Nevertheless, we have not made use of this right, but we endure anything rather than put an obstacle in the way of the gospel of Christ.*

The Gospel Reading
St. Matthew 18:23-35

The Lord said this parable: *"The kingdom of heaven may be compared to a king who wished to settle ac-*

counts with his servants. When he began the reckoning, one was brought to him who owed him ten thousand talents; and as he could not pay, his lord ordered him to be sold, with his wife and children and all that he had, and payment to be made. So the servant fell on his knees, imploring him, 'Lord, have patience with me, and I will pay you everything.' And out of pity for him the lord of that servant released him and forgave him the debt. But that same servant, as he went out, came upon one of his fellow servants who owed him a hundred denarii; and seizing him by the throat he said, 'Pay what you owe.' So his fellow servant fell down and besought him, 'Have patience with me, and I will pay you.' He refused and went and put him in prison till he should pay the debt. When his fellow servants saw what had taken place, they were greatly distressed, and they went and reported to their lord all that had taken place. Then his lord summoned him and said to him, 'You wicked servant! I forgave you all that debt because you besought me; and should not you have had mercy on your fellow servant, as I had mercy on you?' And in anger his lord delivered him to the jailers, till he should pay all his debt. So also my heavenly Father will do to every one of you, if you do not forgive your brother from your heart.

TWELFTH SUNDAY
The Apostolic Reading
I Corinthians 15:1-11

I would remind you, brethren, in what terms I preached to you the gospel, which you received, in which you stand, by which you are saved, if you hold it fast — unless you believed in vain.

For I delivered to you as of first importance what I also received, that Christ died for our sins in accordance with the scriptures, that he was buried, that he was raised on the third day in accordance with the scriptures, and that he appeared to Cephas, then to the twelve. Then he appeared to more than five hundred brethren at one time, most of whom are still alive, though some have fallen asleep. Then he appeared to James, then to all the apostles. Last of all, as to one untimely born, he appeared also to me. For I am the least of the apostles, unfit to be called an apostle, because I persecuted the church of God. But by the grace of God I am what I am, and his grace toward me was not in vain. On the contrary, I worked harder than any of them, though it was not I, but the grace of God which is with me. Whether then it was I or they, so we preach and so you believed.

The Gospel Reading
St. Matthew 19:16-24

At that time, a young man came up to Jesus, kneeling and saying, "Good Teacher, what good deed must I do, to have eternal life?" And he said to him, "Why do you call me good? One there is who is good, and he is Good. If you would enter life, keep the commandments." He said to him, "Which?" And Jesus said, "You shall not kill, You shall not commit adultery, You shall not steal, You shall not bear false witness, Honor your father and mother, and You shall love your neighbor as yourself." The young man said to him, "All these I have observed; what do I still lack?" Jesus said to him, "If you would be perfect, go, sell what you possess and give to the poor, and you will have treasure in heaven; and come, follow me." When the young man heard this he went away sorrowful; for he had great possessions.

And Jesus said to his disciples, "Truly, I say to you, it will be hard for a rich man to enter the kingdom of heaven. Again I tell you, it is easier for a camel to go through the eye of a needle than for a rich man to enter the kingdom of God." When the disciples heard this they were greatly astonished, saying, "Who then can be saved?" But Jesus looked at them and said to them, "With men this is impossible, but with God all things are possible."

THIRTEENTH SUNDAY

The Apostolic Reading
I Corinthians 16:13-24

Brethren, watchful, stand firm in your faith, be courageous, be strong. Let all that you do be done in love.

Now, brethren, you know that the household of Steph'anas were the first converts in Acha'ia, and they have devoted themselves to the service of the saints; I urge you to be subject to such men and to every fellow worker and laborer. I rejoice at the coming of Steph'anas and Fortuna'tus and Acha'icus, because they have made up for your absence; for they refreshed my spirit as well as yours. Give recognition to such men.

The churches of Asia send greetings. Aquila and Prisca, together with the church in their house, send you hearty greetings in the Lord. All the brethren send greetings. Greet one another with a holy kiss.

I, Paul, write this greeting with my own hand. If any one has no love for the Lord, let him be accursed. Our

Lord, come! The grace of the Lord Jesus be with you. My love be with you all in Christ Jesus. Amen.

The Gospel Reading
St. Matthew 21:33-42

The Lord said this parable: "There was a householder who planted a vineyard, and set a hedge around it, and dug a wine press in it, and built a tower, and let it out to tenants, and went into another country. When the season of fruit drew near, he sent his servants to the tenants, to get his fruit; and the tenants took his servants and beat one, killed another, and stoned another. Again he sent other servants, more than the first; and they did the same to them. Afterward he sent his son to them, saying, "They will respect my son.' But when the tenants saw the son, they said to themselves, 'This is the heir; come, let us kill him and have his inheritance.' And they took him and cast him out of the vineyard, and killed him. When therefore the owner of the vineyard comes, what will he do to those tenants?" They said to him, "He will put those wretches to a miserable death, and let out the vineyard to other tenants who will give him the fruits in their seasons."

Jesus said to them, "Have you never read in the scriptures:

'The very stone which the builders rejected has become the head of the corner;

this was the Lord's doing,

and it is marvelous in our eyes'?

FOURTEENTH SUNDAY

The Apostolic Reading
2 Corinthians 1:21-24; 2:1-4

Brethren, it is God who establishes us with you in Christ, and has commissioned us; he has put his seal upon us and given us his Spirit in our hearts as a guarantee.

But I call God to witness against me — it was to spare you that I refrained from coming to Corinth. Not that we lord it over your faith; we work with you for your joy, for you stand firm in your faith. For I made up my mind not to make you another painful visit. For if I cause you pain, who is there to make me glad but the one whom I have pained? And I wrote as I did, so that when I came I might not suffer pain from those who should have made me rejoice, for I felt sure of all of you, that my joy would be the joy of you all. For I wrote you out of much affliction and anguish of heart and with many tears, not to cause you pain but to let you know the abundant love that I have for you.

The Gospel Reading
St. Matthew 22:2-14

The Lord said this parable: "The kingdom of heaven may be compared to a king who gave a marriage feast for his son, and sent his servants to call those who were invited to the marriage feast; but they would not come. Again he sent other servants, saying, 'Tell those who are invited, Behold, I have made ready my dinner, my oxen and my fat calves are killed, and everything is ready; come to the marriage feast.' But they made light of it and went off, one to his farm, another to his business, while the rest seized his servants, treated them shamefully, and killed them. The king was angry, and he sent his troops and destroyed those murderers and burned their city. Then he said to his servants, 'The wedding is ready, but those invited were not worthy. Go therefore to the thoroughfares, and invite to the marriage feast as many as you find.' And those servants went out into the streets and gathered all whom they found, both bad and good; so the wedding hall was filled with guests.

"But when the king came in to look at the guests, he saw there a man who had no wedding garment; and he said to him, 'Friend, how did you get in here without a wedding garment?' And he was speechless. Then the king said to the attendants, 'Bind him hand and foot, and cast him into the outer darkness; there men will weep and gnash their teeth.' For many are called, but few are chosen."

FIFTEENTH SUNDAY

The Apostolic Reading
2 Corinthians 4:6-15

Brethren, it is the God who said, "Let light shine out of darkness," who has shone in our hearts to give the light of the knowledge of the glory of God in the face of Christ.

But we have this treasure in earthen vessels, to show that the transcendent power belongs to God and not to us. We are afflicted in every way, but not crushed; perplexed, but not driven to despair; persecuted, but not forsaken; struck down, but not destroyed; always carrying in the body the death of Jesus, so that the life of Jesus may also be manifested in our bodies. For while we live we are always being given up to death for Jesus' sake, so that the life of Jesus may be manifested in our mortal flesh. So death is at work in us, but life in you.

Since we have the same spirit of faith as he had who wrote, "I believed, and so I spoke," we too believe, and so we speak, knowing that he who raised the Lord Jesus will raise us also with Jesus and bring us with you into his presence. For it is all for your sake, so that as grace extends to more and more people it may increase thanksgiving, to the glory of God.

The Gospel Reading
St. Matthew 22:35-46

At that time a lawyer, asked him a question, to test him. 'Teacher, which is the great commandment in the law?" And he said to him, "You shall love the Lord your God with all your heart, and with all your soul, and with all your mind. This is the great and first commandment. And a second is like it, You shall love your neighbor as yourself. On these two commandments depend all the law and the prophets."

Now while the Pharisees were gathered together, Jesus asked them a question, saying, "What do you think of the Christ? Whose son is he?" They said to him, "The son of David." He said to them, "How is it then that David, inspired by the Spirit, calls him Lord, saying,

'The Lord said to my Lord,

Sit at my right hand,

till I put thy enemies under thy feet'?

If David thus calls him Lord, how is he his son?" And no one was able to answer him a word, nor from

138

that day did any one dare to ask him any more questions.

SIXTEENTH SUNDAY

The Apostolic Reading
2 Corinthians 6:1-10

Brethren, working together with him, we entreat you not to accept the grace of God in vain. For he says, "at the acceptable time I have listened to you, and helped you on the day of salvation". Behold, now is the acceptable time; behold, now is the day of salvation. We put no obstacle in any one's way, so that no fault may be found with our ministry, but as servants of God we commend ourselves in every way: through great endurance, in afflictions, hardships, calamities, beatings, imprisonments, tumults, labors, watching, hunger; by purity, knowledge, forbearance, kindness, the Holy Spirit, genuine love, truthful speech, and the power of God; with the weapons of righteousness for the right hand and for the left; in honor and dishonor, in ill repute and good repute. We are treated as imposters, and yet are true; as unknown, and yet well known; as dying, and behold we live, as punished, and yet not killed; as sorrowful, yet always rejoicing; as poor, yet making many rich; as having nothing, and yet possessing everything.

The Gospel Reading
St. Matthew 25:14-30

The Lord said this parable: "A man going on a journey called his servants and entrusted to them his property; to one he gave five talents, to another two, to another one, to each according to his ability. Then he went away. He who had received the five talents went at once and traded with them; and he made five talents more. So also, he who had the two talents made two talents more. But he who had received the one talent went and dug in the ground and hid his master's money. Now after a long time the master of those servants came and settled accounts with them. And he who had received the five talents came forward, bringing five talents more, saying, 'Master, you delivered to me five talents; here I have made five talents more.' His master said to him, 'Well done, good and faithful servant; you have been faithful over a little, I will set you over much; enter into the joy of your master.' And he also who had the two talents came forward, saying, 'Master, you delivered to me two talents; here I have made two talents more.' His master said to him, 'Well done, good and faithful servant; you have been faithful over a little, I will set you over much; enter into the joy of your master.' He also who had received the one talent came forward, saying, 'Master, I knew you to be a hard man, reaping where you did not sow, and gathering where you did not winnow; so I was afraid, and I went and hid your talent in the ground. Here you have what is yours.' But his master answered him, 'You wicked and slothful servant! You knew that I reap where I have not sowed, and gather where I have not winnowed? Then you ought to have invested my money with the bankers, and at my coming I should have received what was my own with interest. So take the talent from him, and give it to him who has the ten talents. For to every one who has will more be given, and he will have abundance; but from him who has not, even what he has will be taken away. And cast the worthless servant into the outer darkness; there men will weep and gnash their teeth.' As he said these things he cried out: "He who has ears to hear, let him hear!"

SEVENTEENTH SUNDAY

The Apostolic Reading
2 Corinthians 6:16-18; 7:1-2

Brethren, what agreement has the temple of God with idols? For we are the temple of the living God; as God said,

"I will live in them and move among them,
and I will be their God,
and they shall be my people.
Therefore come out from them and be separate
from them, says the Lord,
and touch nothing unclean;
then I will welcome you,
and I will be a father to you,
and you shall be my sons and daughters,
says the Lord Almighty."

Since we have these promises, beloved, let us cleanse ourselves from every defilement of body and spirit, and make holiness perfect in the fear of God.

Open your hearts to us; we have wronged no one, we have corrupted no one, we have taken advantage of no one.

The Gospel Reading
St. Matthew 15-21-28

At that time, Jesus went to the district of Tyre and Sidon. And behold, a Canaanite woman from that region came out and cried, "Have mercy on me, O Lord,

Son of David; my daughter is severely possessed by a demon." But he did not answer her a word, And his disciples came and begged him, saying, "Send her away, for she is crying after us." He answered, "I was sent only to the lost sheep of the house of Israel." But she came and knelt before him, saying, "Lord, help me." And he answered, "It is not fair to take the children's bread and throw it to the dogs." She said, "Yes, Lord, yet even the dogs eat the crumbs that fall from their master's table." Then Jesus answered her, "O woman, great is your faith! Be it done for you as you desire." And her daughter was healed instantly.

EIGHTEENTH SUNDAY
The Apostolic Reading
2 Corinthians 9:6-11

Brethren, the point is this: he who sows sparingly will also reap sparingly, and he who sows bountifully will also reap bountifully. Each one must do as he has made up his mind, not reluctantly or under compulsion, for God loves a cheerful giver. And God is able to provide you with every blessing in abundance, so that you may always have enough of everything and may provide in abundance for every good work. As it is written,

"He scatters abroad, he gives to the poor;
his righteousness endures for ever."

He who supplies seed to the sower and bread for food will supply and multiply your resources and increase the harvest of your righteousness. You will be enriched in every way for great generosity, which through us will produce thanksgiving to God.

The Gospel Reading
St. Luke 5:1-11

At that time Jesus was standing by the lake of Gennesaret. And he saw two boats by the lake; but the fishermen had gone out of them and were washing their nets. Getting into one of the boats, which was Simon's, he asked him to put out a little from the land. And he sat down and taught the people from the boat. And when he had ceased speaking, he said to Simon, Put out into the deep and let down your nets for a catch." And Simon answered, "Master, we toiled all night and took nothing! But at your word I will let down the nets." And when they had done this, they enclosed a great shoal of fish; and as their nets were breaking, they beckoned to their partners in the other boat to come and help them. And they came and filled both the boats, so that they began to sink. But when Simon Peter saw it, he fell down at Jesus, knees, saying, "Depart from me, for I am a sinful man, O Lord." For he was astonished, and all that were with him, at the catch of fish which they had taken; and so also were James and John, sons of Zebedee, who were partners with Simon. And Jesus said to Simon, "Do not be afraid; henceforth you will be catching men." And when they had brought their boats to land, they left everything and followed him.

NINETEENTH SUNDAY

The Apostolic Reading
2 Corinthians 11:31-33; 12:1-9

Brethren, the God and Father of the Lord Jesus, he who is blessed for ever, knows that I do not lie. At

Damascus, the governor under king Aretas guarded the city of Damascus in order to seize me, but I was let down in a basket through a window in the wall, and escaped his hands. I must boast; there is nothing to be gained by it, but I will go on to visions and revelations of the Lord. I know a man in Christ who fourteen years ago was caught up to the third heaven — whether in the body or out of the body I do not know, God knows. And I know that this man was caught up into paradise — whether in the body or out of the body I do not know, God knows — and he heard things that cannot be told, which man may not utter. On behalf of this man I will boast, but on my own behalf I will not boast, except of my weaknesses. Though if I wish to boast, I shall not be a fool, for I shall be speaking the truth. But I refrain from it, so that no one may think more of me than he sees in me or hears from me. And to keep me from being too elated by the abundance of revelations, a thorn was given me in the flesh, a messenger of Satan, to harass me, to keep me from being too elated. Three times I besought the Lord about this, that it should leave me; but he said to me, "My grace is sufficient for you, for my power is made perfect in weakness". I will all the more gladly boast of my weaknesses, that the power of Christ may rest upon me.

The Gospel Reading
St. Luke 6:31-36

The Lord said: "As you wish that men would do to you, do so to them.

"If you love those who love you, what credit is that to you? For even sinners love those who love them. And if you do good to those who do good to you, what credit is that to you? For even sinners do the same.

144

And if you lend to those from whom you hope to receive, what credit is that to you? Even sinners lend to sinners, to receive as much again. But love your enemies, and do good, and lend, expecting nothing in return; and your reward will be great, and you will be sons of the Most High; for he is kind to the ungrateful and the selfish. Be merciful, even as your Father is merciful.

TWENTIETH SUNDAY

The Apostolic Reading
Galatians 1:11-19

Brethren, I would have you know that the gospel which was preached by me is not man's gospel. For I did not receive it from man, nor was I taught it, but it came through a revelation of Jesus Christ. For you have heard of my former life in Judaism, how I persecuted the church of God violently and tried to destroy it; and I advanced in Judaism beyond many of my own age among my people, so extremely jealous was I for the traditions of my fathers. But when he who had set me apart before I was born, and had called me through his grace, was pleased to reveal his Son to me, in order that I might preach him among the Gentiles, I did not confer with flesh and blood, nor did I go up to Jerusalem to those who were apostles before me, but I went away into Arabia; and again I returned to Damascus. Then after three years I went up to Jerusalem to visit Cephas, and remained with him fifteen days. But I saw none of the other apostles except James the Lord's brother.

The Gospel Reading
St. Luke 7:11-16

At that time Jesus went to a city called Na'in, and his disciples and a great crowd went with him. As he drew near to the gate of the city, behold, a man who had died was being carried out, the only son of his mother, and a large crowd from the city was with her. And when the Lord saw her, he had compassion on her and said to her, "Do not weep." And he came and touched the bier, and the bearers stood still. And he said, "Young man, I say to you, arise." And the dead man sat up, and began to speak. And he gave him to his mother. Fear seized them all; and they glorified God, saying, "A great prophet has arisen among us!" and "God has visited his people!"

TWENTY-FIRST SUNDAY

The Apostolic Reading
Galatians 2:16-20

Brethren, who know that a man is not justified by faith in Christ, even we have believed in Christ Jesus, in order to be justified by faith in Christ, and not by works of the law, because by works of the law shall no one be justified. But if, in our endeavor to be justified in Christ, we ourselves were found to be sinners, is Christ then an agent of sin? Certainly not! But if I build up again those things which I tore down, then I prove myself a transgressor. For I through the law died to the law, that I might live to God. I have been crucified with Christ; it is no longer I who live, but Christ who lives in me; and the life I now live in the flesh I live by faith in the Son of God, who loved me and gave himself for me.

The Gospel Reading
St. Luke 8:5-15

The Lord said this parable: "A sower went out to sow his seed; and as he sowed, some fell along the path, and was trodden under foot, and the birds of the air devoured it. And some fell on the rock; and as it grew up, it withered away, because it had no moisture. And some fell among thorns; and the thorns grew with it and choked it. And some fell into good soil and grew, and yielded a hundredfold."

And when his disciples asked him what this parable meant, he said, "To you it has been given to know the secrets of the kingdom of God; but for others they are in parables, so that seeing they may not see, and hearing they may not understand. Now the parable is this: The seed is the word of God. The ones along the path are those who have heard; then the devil comes and takes away the word from their hearts, that they may not believe and be saved. And the ones on the rock are those who, when they hear the word, receive it with joy; but these have no root, they believe for a while and in time of temptation fall away. And as for what fell among the thorns, they are those who hear, but as they go on their way they are choked by the cares and riches and pleasures of life, and their fruit does not mature. And as for that in the good soil, they are those who, hearing the word, hold it fast in an honest and good heart, and bring forth fruit with patience. As he said these things, he cried out "He who has ears to hear, let him hear."

TWENTY-SECOND SUNDAY

The Apostolic Reading
Galatians 6:11-18

Brethren, see with what large letters I am writing to you with my own hand. It is those who want to make a good showing in the the flesh that would compel you to be circumcised, and only in order that they may not be persecuted for the cross of Christ. For even those who receive circumcision do not themselves keep the law, but they desire to have you circumcised that they may glory in your flesh. But far be it from me to glory except in the cross of our Lord Jesus Christ, by which the world has been crucified to me, and I to the world. For neither circumcision counts for anything, nor uncircumcision, but a new creation. Peace and mercy be upon all who walk by this rule, upon the Israel of God.

Henceforth let no man trouble me; for I bear on my body the marks of Jesus.

The grace of our Lord Jesus Christ be with your spirit, brethren. Amen.

The Gospel Reading
St. Luke 16:19-31

The Lord said: "There was a rich man, who was clothed in purple and fine linen and who feasted sumptuously every day. And at his gate lay a poor man named Lazarus, full of sores, who desired to be fed with what fell from the rich man's table; moreover the dogs came and licked his sores. The poor man died and was carried by the angels to Abraham's bosom. The rich man also died and was buried; and in Hades, being in torment, he lifted up his eyes, and saw Abraham far off and Lazarus in his bosom. And he called out, 'Father Abraham, have mercy upon me, and send Lazarus to dip the end of his finger in water and cool my tongue; for I am in anguish in this fllame.' But Abraham said, 'Son, remember that you in your lifetime received your good things, and Lazarus in like manner evil things; but now he is comforted here, and you are in anguish. And besides all this, between us and you a great chasm has been fixed, in order that those who would pass from here to you may not be able, and none may cross from there to us.' And he said, 'Then I beg you, father, to send him to my father's house, for I have five brothers, so that he may warn them, lest they also come into this place of torment.' But Abraham said, 'They have Moses, and the prophets; let them hear them.' And he said, 'No, father Abraham; but if some one goes to them from the dead, they will repent.' He said to him, 'If they do not hear Moses and the prophets, neither will they be convinced if some one should rise from the dead.' "

TWENTY-THIRD SUNDAY

The Apostolic Reading
Ephesians 2:4-10

Brethren, God, who is rich in mercy, out of the great love with which he loved us, even when we were dead through our trespasses, made us alive together with Christ (by grace you have been saved), and raised us up with him in the heavenly places in Christ Jesus, that in the coming ages he might show the immeasurable riches of his grace in kindness toward us in

Christ Jesus. For by grace you have been saved through faith; and this is not your own doing, it is the gift of God — not because of works, lest any man should boast. For we are his workmanship, created in Christ Jesus for good works, which God prepared beforehand, that we should walk in them.

The Gospel Reading
St. Luke 8:26-39

At that time, as Jesus arrived at the country of the Gerasenes, there met him a man from the city who had demons; for a long time he had worn no clothes, and he lived not in a house but among the tombs. When he saw Jesus, he cried out and fell down before him, and said with a loud voice, "What have you to do with me, Jesus, Son of the Most High God? I beseech you, do not torment me."

For he had commanded the unclean spirit to come out of the man. (For many a time it had seized him; he was kept under guard, and bound with chains and fetters, but he broke the bonds and was driven by the demon into the desert.) Jesus then asked him, "What is your name?" And he said, "Legion"; for many demons had entered him. And they begged him not to command them to depart into the abyss. Now a large herd of swine was feeding there on the hillside; and they begged him to let them enter these. So he gave them leave. Then the demons came out of the man and entered the swine, and the herd rushed down the steep bank into the lake and were drowned.

When the herdsmen saw what happened, they fled, and told it in the city and in the country. Then people went out to see what had happened, and they came to Jesus, and found the man from whom the demons had gone, sitting at the feet of Jesus, clothed and in his right mind; and they were afraid. And those who had seen it told them how he who had been possessed with demons was healed. Then all the people of the surrounding country of the Gerasenes asked him to depart from them; for they were seized with great fear; so he got into the boat and returned. The man from whom the demons had gone begged that he might be with him; but he sent him away, saying, "Return to your home, and declare how much God has done for you." And he went away, proclaiming throughout the whole city how much Jesus had done for him.

TWENTY-FOURTH SUNDAY

The Apostolic Reading
Ephesians 2:14-22

Brethren, he is our peace, who has made us both one, and has broken down the dividing wall of hostility, by abolishing in his flesh the law of commandments and ordinances, that he might create in himself one new man in place of the two, so making peace, and might reconcile us both to God in one body through the cross, thereby bringing the hostility to an end. And he came and preached peace to you who were far off and peace to those who were near; for through him we both have access in one Spirit to the Father. So then you are no longer strangers and so-journers, but you are fellow citizens with the saints and members of the household of God, built upon the foundation of the apostles and prophets, Christ Jesus himself being cornerstone, in whom the whole structure is joined together and grows into a holy temple in the Lord; in whom you also are built into it for a dwelling place of God in the Spirit.

The Gospel Reading
St. Luke 8:41-56

At that time, there came to Jesus a man named Jairus, who was a ruler of the synagogue; and falling at Jesus' feet he besought him to come to his house, for he had an only daughter, about twelve years of age, and she was dying.

As he went, the people pressed round him. And a woman who had had a flow of blood for twelve years and had spent all her living upon physicians and could not be healed by any one, came up behind him, and touched the fringe of his garment; and immediately her flow of blood ceased. And Jesus said, "Who was it that touched me?" When all denied it, Peter said, "Master, the multitudes surround you and press upon you!" But Jesus said, "Some one touched me; for I perceive that power has gone forth from me." And when the woman saw that she was not hidden, she came trembling, and falling down before him declared in the presence of all the people why she had touched him, and how she had been immediately healed. And he said to her, "Daughter, your faith has made you well; go in peace."

While he was still speaking, a man from the ruler's house came and said, "Your daughter is dead; do not trouble the Teacher any more." But Jesus on hearing this answered him, "Do not fear; only believe, and she shall be well." And when he came to the house, he permitted no one to enter with him, except Peter and John and James, and the father and mother of the child. And all were weeping and bewailing her; but he

said, " Do not weep; for she is not dead but sleeping."
And they laughed at him, knowing that she was dead.
But taking her by the hand he called, saying, "Child,
arise." And her spirit returned, and she got up at once;
and he directed that something should be given her to
eat. And her parents were amazed; but he charged
them to tell no one what had happened.

TWENTY-FIFTH SUNDAY

The Apostolic Reading
Ephesians 4:1-7

Brethren, I therefore, a prisoner for the Lord, beg
you to lead a life worthy of the calling to which you
have been called, with all lowliness and meekness,
with patience, forbearing one another in love, eager to
maintain the unity of the spirit in the bond of peace.
There is one body and one spirit, just as you were
called to the one hope that belongs to your call, one
Lord, one faith, one baptism, one God and Father of
us all, who is above all and through all and in all. But
grace was given to each of us according to the measure
of Christ's gift.

The Gospel Reading
St. Luke 10:25-37

At that time, a lawyer stood up to put Jesus to the
test, saying, "Teacher, what shall I do to inherit eternal
life?" He said to him, "What is written in the law?
How do you read?" And he answered, "You shall love
the Lord your God with all your heart, and with all
your soul, and with all your strength, and with all your
mind; and your neighbor as yourself." And he said

153

to him, "You have answered right; do this, and you will live."

But he, desiring to justify himself, said to Jesus, "And who is my neighbor?" Jesus replied, "A man was going down from Jerusalem to Jericho, and he fell among robbers, who stripped him and beat him, and departed, leaving him half dead. Now by chance a priest was going down that road; and when he saw him he passed by on the other side. So likewise a Levite, when he came to the place and saw him, passed by on the other side. But a Samaritan, as he journeyed, came to where he was; and when he saw him, he had compassion, and went to him and bound up his wounds, pouring on oil and wine; then he set him on his own beast and brought him to an inn, and took care of him. And the next day he took out two denarii and gave them to the innkeeper, saying, 'Take care of him; and whatever more you spend, I will repay you when I come back.' Which of these three, do you think, proved neighbor to the man who fell among the robbers?" He said, "The one who showed mercy on him." And Jesus said to him, "Go and do likewise."

TWENTY-SIXTH SUNDAY

The Apostolic Reading
Ephesians 5:8-20

Once you were darkness, but now you are light in the Lord; walk as children of light (for the fruit of light is found in all that is good and right and true), and try to learn what is pleasing to the Lord. Take no part in the unfruitful works of darkness, but instead expose them. For it is a shame even to speak of the things that they do in secret; but when anything is exposed by the light it becomes visible, for anything that becomes visible is light. Therefore it is said,

"Awake, O sleeper, and arise from the dead, and Christ shall give you light."

Look carefully then how you walk, not as unwise men but as wise, making the most of the time, because the days are evil. Therefore do not be foolish, but understand what the will of the Lord is. And do not get drunk with wine, for that is debauchery; but be filled with the Spirit, addressing one another in psalms and hymns and spiritual songs, singing and making melody to the Lord with all your heart, always and for everything giving thanks in the name of our Lord Jesus Christ to God the Father.

The Gospel Reading
St. Luke 12:16-21

The Lord said this parable: "The land of a rich man brought forth plentifully; and he thought to himself, 'What shall I do, for I have nowhere to store my crops?' And he said, 'I will do this: I will pull down my barns, and build larger ones; and there I will store all my grain and my goods. And I will say to my soul, Soul, you have ample goods laid up for many years; take your ease, eat, drink, be merry.' But God said to him, 'Fool! This night your soul is required of you; and the things you have prepared, whose will they be? So is he who lays up treasure for himself, and is not rich toward God." As he said these things, he cried out: "He who has ears to hear, let him hear."

TWENTY-SEVENTH SUNDAY

The Apostolic Reading
Ephesians 6:10-17

Finally, be strong in the Lord and in the strength of his might. Put on the whole armor of God, that you may be able to stand against the wiles of the devil. For we are not contending against flesh and blood, but against the principalities, against the powers, against the world rulers of this present darkness, against the spiritual hosts of wickedness in the heavenly places. Therefore take the whole armor of God, that you may be able to withstand in the evil day, and having done all, to stand. Stand therefore, having girded your loins with truth, and having put on the breastplate of righteousness, and having shod your feet with the equipment of the gospel of peace; besides all these, taking the shield of faith, with which you can quench all the flaming darts of the evil one. And take the helmet of salvation, and the sword of the Spirit, which is the word of God.

The Gospel Reading
St. Luke 13:10-17

At that time, Jesus was teaching in one of the synagogues on the sabbath. And there was a woman who had a spirit of infirmity for eighteen years; she was bent over and could not fully straighten herself. And when Jesus saw her, he called her and said to her, "Woman, you are freed from your infirmity." And he laid his hands upon her, and immediately she was made straight, and she praised God. But the ruler of the synagogue, indignant because Jesus had healed on the sabbath, said to the people, "There are six days on which work ought to be done; come on those days and be healed, and not on the sabbath day." Then the Lord answered him, "You hypocrites! Does not each of you on the sabbath untie his ox or his ass from the manger, and lead it away to water it? And ought not this woman, a daughter of Abraham whom Satan bound for eighteen years, be loosed from this bond on the sabbath day?" As he said this, all his adversaries were put to shame; and all the people rejoiced at all the glorious things that were done by him.

TWENTY-EIGHTH SUNDAY

The Apostolic Reading
Colossians 1:12-18

Brethren, giving thanks to the Father, who has qualified us to share in the inheritance of the saints in light. He has delivered us from the dominion of darkness and transferred us to the kingdom of his beloved Son, in whom we have redemption, the forgiveness of sins.

He is the image of the invisible God, the first-born of all creation; for in him all things were created, in heaven and on earth, visible and invisible, whether thrones or dominions or principalities or authorities— all things were created through him and for him. He is before all things, and in him all things hold together. He is the head of the body, the church; he is the beginning, the first-born from the dead, that in everything he might be pre-eminent.

The Gospel Reading
St. Luke 14:16-24

The Lord said this parable: "A man once gave a great banquet, and invited many; and at the time for the banquet he sent his servant to say to those who had been invited, 'Come; for all is now ready.' But they all alike began to make excuses. The first said to him, 'I have bought a field, and I must go out and see it; I pray you, have me excused.' And another said, 'I have bought five yoke of oxen, and I go to examine them; I pray you, have me excused.' And another said, 'I have married a wife, and therefore I cannot come.' So the servant came and reported this to his master. Then the householder in anger said to his servant, 'Go out quickly to the streets and lanes of the city, and bring in the poor and maimed and blind and lame.' And the servant said, 'Sir, what you commanded has been done, and still there is room.' And the master said to the servant, 'Go out to the highways and hedges, and compel people to come in, that my house may be filled. For I tell you, none of those men who were invited shall taste my banquet. For many are called, but few are chosen.'"

TWENTY-NINTH SUNDAY

The Apostolic Reading
Colossians 3:4-11

Brethren, when Christ who is our life appears, then you also will appear with him in glory.

Put to death therefore what is earthly in you; fornication, impurity passions, evil desire, and covetousness, which is idolatry. On account of these the wrath of God is coming. In these you once walked, when you lived in them. But now put them all away: anger, wrath, malice, slander, and foul talk from your mouth. Do not lie to one another, seeing that you have put off the old nature with its practices and have put on the new nature, which is being renewed in knowledge after the image of its creator. Here there cannot be Greek and Jew, circumcised and uncircumcised, barbarian, Scyth'ian, slave, free man, but Christ is all, and in all.

The Gospel Reading
St. Luke 17-12-19

At that time, as Jesus entered a village, he was met by ten lepers, who stood at a distance and lifted up their voices and said, "Jesus, Master, have mercy on us." When he saw them he said to them, "Go and show yourselves to the priests." And as they went they were cleansed. Then one of them, when he saw that he was healed, turned back, praising God with a loud voice; and he fell on his face at Jesus' feet, giving him thanks. Now he was a Samaritan. Then said Jesus, "Were not ten cleansed? Where are the nine? Was no one found to return and give praise to God except this foreigner?" And he said to him, "Rise and go your way; your faith has made you well."

THIRTIETH SUNDAY

The Apostolic Reading
Colossians 3-12-16

Put on then, as God's chosen ones, holy and beloved, compassion, kindness, lowliness, meekness, and patience, forbearing one another and, if one has a complaint against another, forgiving each other; as the Lord has forgiven you, so you also must forgive. And above all these put on love, which binds everything together in perfect harmony. And let the peace of Christ rule in your hearts, to which indeed you were called in the one body. And be thankful. Let the word of Christ dwell in you richly, teach and admonish one another in all wisdom, and sing psalms and hymns and spiritual songs with thankfulness in your hearts to God.

The Gospel Reading
St. Luke 18:18-27

At that time, a ruler came to Jesus and asked him, "Good Teacher, what shall I do to inherit eternal life?" And Jesus said to him, "Why do you call me good? No one is good but God alone. You know the commandments: 'Do not commit adultery, Do not kill, Do not steal, Do not bear false witness, Honor your father and mother.'" And he said, "All these I have observed from my youth." And when Jesus heard it, he said to him, "One thing you still lack. Sell all that you have and distribute to the poor, and you will have treasure in heaven; and come, follow me." But when he heard this he became sad, for he was very rich. Jesus looking at him said, "How hard it is for those who have riches to enter the kingdom of God! For it is easier for a camel to go through the eye of a needle than for a rich man to enter the kingdom of God." Those who heard it said, "Then who can be saved?" But he said, "What is impossible with men is possible with God."

160

THIRTY-FIRST SUNDAY

The Apostolic Reading
I Timothy 1:15-17

Brethren, the saying is sure and worthy of full acceptance, that Christ Jesus came into the world to save sinners. And I am the foremost of sinners; but I received mercy for this reason, that in me, as the foremost, Jesus Christ might display his perfect patience for an example to those who were to believe in him for eternal life. To the King of ages, immortal, invisible, the only God, be honor and glory for ever and ever. Amen.

The Gospel Reading
St. Luke 18:35-43

At that time, as Jesus drew near to Jericho, a blind man was sitting by the roadside begging; and hearing a multitude going by, he inquired what this meant. They told him, "Jesus of Nazareth is passing by." And he cried, "Jesus, Son of David, have mercy on me!" And those who were in front rebuked him, telling him to be silent; but he cried out all the more, "Son of David, have mercy on me!" And Jesus stopped, and commanded him to be brought to him; and when he came near, he asked him, "What do you want me to do for you?" He said, "Lord, let me receive my sight." And Jesus said to him, "Receive your sight; your faith has made you well." And immediately he received his sight and followed him, glorifying God; and all the people, when they saw it, gave praise to God.

THIRTY-SECOND SUNDAY

The Apostolic Reading
I Timothy 4:9-15

Brethren, the saying is sure and worthy of full acceptance. For to this end we toil and strive, because we
have our hope set on the living God, who is the Savior
of all men, especially of those who believe.

Command and teach these things. Let no one despise
your youth, but set the believers an example in speech
and conduct, in love, in faith, in purity. Till I come,
attend to the public reading of scripture, to preaching,
to teaching. Do not neglect the gift you have, which
was given you by prophetic utterance when the council of elders laid their hands upon you. Practice these
duties, devote yourself to them, so that all may see
your progress.

The Gospel Reading
St. Luke 19:1-10

At that time, Jesus entered Jericho and was passing
through. And there was a man named Zacchaeus; he
was a chief tax collector, and rich. And he sought to
see who Jesus was, but could not, on account of the
crowd, because he was small of stature. So he ran on
ahead and climbed up into a sycamore tree to see him,
for he was to pass that way. And when Jesus came to
the place, he looked up and said to him, "Zacchaeus,
make haste and come down; for I must stay at your
house today." So he made haste and came down, and
received him joyfully. And when they saw it they all
murmured, "He has gone in to be the guest of a man
who is a sinner." And Zacchaeus stood and said to the
Lord, "Behold, Lord, the half of my goods I give to

the poor; and if I have defrauded any one of anything, I restore it fourfold." And Jesus said to him, "Today salvation has come to this house, since he also is a son of Abraham. For the Son of man came to seek and to save the lost."

SUNDAY OF THE FOREFATHERS

The Apostolic Reading
Colossians 3:4-11

Brethren, when Christ who is our life appears, then you also will appear with him in glory. Put to death therefore what is earthly in you: immorality, impurity, passion, evil desire, and covetousness, which is idolatry. On account of these the wrath of God is coming. In these you once walked when you lived in them. But now put them all away: anger, wrath, malice, slander, and foul talk from your mouth. Do not lie to one another, seeing that you have put off the old nature with its practices and have put on the new nature, which is being renewed in knowledge after the image of its creator. Here there cannot be Greek and Jew, circumcised, uncircumcised, barbarian, Scythian, slave, free man, but Christ is all, and in all.

The Gospel Reading
St. Luke 14:16-24

The Lord said: A man once gave a great banquet, and invited many; and at the time for the banquet he sent his servants to say to those who had been invited, "Come; for all is now ready." But they all alike began to make excuses. The first said to him, "I have bought a field, and I must go out and see it; I pray you, have me excused." And another said, "I have bought five yoke of oxen, and I go to examine them; I pray you, have me excused." And another said, "I have married a wife, and therefore I cannot come." So the servant came and reported this to his master. Then the householder in anger said to his servant, "Go out quickly to the streets and lanes of the city, and bring in the poor and maimed and blind and lame." And the servant said, "Sir, what you commanded has been done, and still there is room." And the master said to the servant, "Go out to the highways and hedges, and compel people to come in, that my house may be filled. For I tell you, none of those men who were invited shall taste my banquet. For many are called, but few are chosen."

SUNDAY BEFORE CHRISTMAS
The Apostolic Reading
Hebrews 11:9-10; 32-40

Brethren, by faith Abraham sojourned in the land of promise, as in a foreign land, living in tents with Isaac and Jacob, heirs with him of the same promise. For he looked forward to the city which has foundations, whose builder and maker is God. And what more shall I say? For time will fail me to tell of Gideon, Barak, Samson, Jephthah, of David and Samuel and the prophets — who through faith conquered kingdoms, and forced justice, received promises, stopped the mouths of lions, quenched raging fire, escaped the edge of the sword, won strength out of weakness, became mighty in war, put foreign armies to flight. Women received their dead by resurrection. Some were tortured, refusing to accept release, that they might rise again to a better life. Others suffered mocking and scourging, and even chains and imprisonment. They were stoned, they were sawn in two, they were killed with the sword; they went about in skins of sheep and goats, destitute, afflicted, ill-treated (of whom the world is not worthy) wandering over deserts and mountains, and in dens and caves of the earth. And all these, though well attested by their faith, did not receive what was promised, since God had foreseen something better for us, that apart from us they should not be made perfect.

The Gospel Reading
St. Matthew 1:1-25

The book of the genealogy of Jesus Christ, the son of David, the son of Abraham.

Abraham was the father of Isaac, and Isaac the father of Jacob, and Jacob the father of Judah and his brothers, and Judah the father of Perez and Zerah by Tamar, and Perez the father of Hezron, and Hezron the father of Ram, and Ram the father of Amminadab, and Amminadab the father of Nahshon, and Nahshon the father of Salmon, and Salmon the father of Boaz by Rahab, and Boaz the father of Obed by Ruth, and Obed the father of Jesse, and Jesse the father of David the king.

And David was the father of Solomon by the wife of Uriah, and Solomon the father of Rehoboam, and Rehoboam the father of Abijah, and Abijah the father of Asa, and Asa the father of Jehoshaphat, and Jehoshaphat the father of Joram, and Joram the father of Uzziah, and Uzziah the father of Jotham, and Jotham the father of Ahaz, and Ahaz the father of Hezekiah, and Hezekiah the father of Manasseh, and Manasseh the father of Amos, and Amos the father of Josiah, and Josiah the father of Jechoniah and his brothers, at the time of the deportation to Babylon.

And after the deportation to Babylon: Jechoniah was the father of Shealtiel, and Shealtiel the father of Zerubbabel, and Zerubbabel the father of Abiud, and Abiud the father of Eliakim, and Eliakim the father of Azor, and Azor the father of Zadok, and Zadok the father of Achim, and Achim the father of Eliud, and Eliud the father of Eleazar, and Eleazar the father of Matthan, and Matthan the father of Jacob, and Jacob the father of Joseph, the husband of Mary, of whom Jesus was born, who is called Christ.

So all the generations from Abraham to David were fourteen generations, and from David to the deportation to Babylon fourteen generations, and from the deportation to Babylon to the Christ fourteen generations.

Now the birth of Jesus Christ took place in this way. When his mother Mary had been betrothed to Joseph, before they came together she was found to be with child of the Holy Spirit; and her husband Joseph, being a just man and unwilling to put her to shame, resolved to send her away quietly. But as he considered this, behold, an angel of the Lord appeared to him in a dream, saying, "Joseph, son of David, do not fear to take Mary your wife, for that which is conceived in her is of the Holy Spirit; she will bear a son, and you shall call his name Jesus, for he will save his people from their sins." All this took place to fulfil what the Lord had spoken by the prophet:

"Behold, a virgin shall conceive and bear a son,
and his name shall be called Emmanuel"
(which means, God with us). When Joseph woke from
sleep, he did as the angel of the Lord commanded him;
he took his wife, but knew her not until she had borne
a son; and he called his name Jesus.

CHRISTMAS DAY

The Apostolic Reading
Galatians 4:4-7

Brethren, when the time had fully come, God sent
forth his Son, born of woman, born under the law, to
redeem those who were under the law, so that we
might receive adoption as sons. And because you are
sons, God has sent the Spirit of his Son into our hearts,
crying, "Abba! Father!" So through God you are no
longer a slave but a son, and if a son then an heir.

The Gospel Reading
St. Matthew 2:1-12

When Jesus was born in Bethlehem of Judea in the
days of Herod the king, behold, wise men from the
East came to Jerusalem, saying, "Where is he who has
been born king of the Jews? For we have seen his star
in the East, and have come to worship him." When
Herod the king heard this, he was troubled, and all
Jerusalem with him; and assembling all the chief
priests and scribes of the people, he inquired of them
where the Christ was to be born. They told him, "In
Bethlehem of Judea; for so it is written by the prophet:

'And you, O Bethlehem, in the land of Judah,
are by no means least among the rulers of Judah;

for from you shall come a ruler
who will govern my people Israel.'"

Then Herod summoned the wise men secretly and ascertained from them what time the star appeared; and he sent them to Bethlehem, saying, "Go and search diligently for the child, and when you have found him bring me word, that I too may come and worship him." When they had heard the king they went their way; and lo, the star which they had seen in the East went before them, till it came to rest over the place where the child was. When they saw the star, they rejoiced exceedingly with great joy; and going into the house they saw the child with Mary his mother, and they fell down and worshiped him. Then, opening their treasures, they offered him gifts, gold and frankincense and myrrh. And being warned in a dream not to return to Herod, they departed to their own country by another way.

SUNDAY AFTER CHRISTMAS

The Apostolic Reading
Galatians 1:11-19

For I would have you know, brethren, that the gospel which was preached by me is not man's gospel. For I did not receive it from man, nor was I taught it, but it came through a revelation of Jesus Christ. For you have heard of my former life in Judaism, how I persecuted the church of God violently and tried to destroy it; and I advanced in Judaism beyond many of my own age among my people, so extremely zealous was I for the traditions of my fathers. But when he who had set me apart before I was born, and had called me through his grace, was pleased to reveal his Son to me, in order that I might preach him among the Gentiles, I did not confer with flesh and blood, nor did I go up to Jerusalem to those who were apostles before me, but I went away into Arabia; and again I returned to Damascus.

Then after three years I went up to Jerusalem to visit Cephas, and remained with him fifteen days. But I saw none of the other apostles except James the Lord's brother.

The Gospel Reading
St. Matthew 2:13-23

When the Magi had departed, behold, an angel of the Lord appeared to Joseph in a dream and said, "Rise, take the child and his mother, and flee to Egypt, and remain there till I tell you; for Herod is about to search for the child, to destroy him." And he rose and took the child and his mother by night, and departed to Egypt, and remained there until the death of Herod. This was to fulfil what the Lord has spoken by the prophet "Out of Egypt have I called my son."

Then Herod, when he saw that he had been tricked by the wise men, was in a furious rage, and he sent and killed all the male children in Bethlehem and in all that region who were two years old or under, according to the time which he had ascertained from the wise men. Then was fulfilled what was spoken by the prophet Jeremiah:

"A voice was heard in Ramah,
wailing and loud lamentation,
Rachel weeping for her children;
she refused to be consoled,
because they were no more."

But when Herod died, behold, an angel of the Lord appeared in a dream to Joseph in Egypt, saying, "Rise, take the child and his mother, and go to the land of Israel, for those who sought the child's life are dead." And he rose and took the child and his mother, and went to the land of Israel. But when he heard that Archelaus reigned over Judea in place of his father Herod, he was afraid to go there, and being warned in a dream he withdrew to the district of Galilee. And he went and dwelt in a city called Nazareth, that what was spoken by the prophets might be fulfilled, "He shall be called a Nazarene."

SUNDAY BEFORE EPIPHANY

The Apostolic Reading
2 Timothy 4:5-8

As for you, always be steady, endure suffering, do the work of an evangelist, fulfil your ministry.

For I am already on the point of being sacrificed; the time of my departure has come. I have fought the good fight, I have finished the race, I have kept the faith. Henceforth there is laid up for me the crown of righteousness, which the Lord, the righteous judge, will award to me on that Day, and not only to me but also to all who have loved his appearing.

The Gospel Reading
St. Mark 1:1-8

The beginning of the gospel of Jesus Christ, the Son of God.

As it is written in Isaiah the prophet,
"Behold, I send my messenger before thy face,

who shall prepare thy way;
the voice of one crying in the wilderness:
Prepare the way of the Lord,
make his paths straight—"

John the baptizer appeared in the wilderness, preaching a baptism of repentance for the forgiveness of sins. And there went out to him all the country of Judea, and all the people of Jerusalem; and they were baptized by him in the river Jordan, confessing their sins. Now John was clothed with camel's hair, and had a leather girdle around his waist, and ate locusts and wild honey. And he preached, saying, "After me comes he who is mightier than I, the thong of whose sandals I am not worthy to stoop down and untie. I have baptized you with water; but he will baptize you with the Holy Spirit."

EPIPHANY DAY

The Apostolic Reading
Titus 2:11-14; 3:4-7

For the grace of God has appeared for the salvation of all men, training us to renounce irreligion and worldly passions, and to live sober, upright, and godly lives in this world, awaiting our blessed hope, the appearing of the glory of our great God and Savior Jesus Christ, who gave himself for us to redeem us from all iniquity and to purify for himself a people of his own who are zealous for good deeds; when the goodness and loving kindness of God our Savior appeared, he saved us, not because of deeds done by us in righteousness, but in virtue of his own mercy, by the washing of regeneration and renewal in the Holy

171

Spirit, which he poured out upon us richly through Jesus Christ our Savior, so that we might be justified by his grace and become heirs in hope of eternal life.

The Gospel Reading
St. Matthew 3:13-17

Then Jesus came from Galilee to the Jordan to John, to be baptized by him. John would have prevented him, saying, "I need to be baptized by you, and do you come to me?" But Jesus answered him, "Let it be so now; for thus it is fitting for us to fulfil all righteousness." Then he consented. And when Jesus was baptized, he went up immediately from the water, and behold, the heavens were opened and he saw the Spirit of God descending like a dove, and alighting on him; and lo, a voice from heaven, saying, "This is my beloved Son, with whom I am well pleased."

SUNDAY AFTER EPIPHANY

The Apostolic Reading
Ephesians 4:7-13

Grace was given to each of us according to the measure of Christ's gift. Therefore it is said,
"When he ascended on high he led a host of captives, and he gave gifts to men."
(In saying, "He ascended," what does it mean but that he had also descended into the lower parts of the earth? He who descended is he who also ascended far above all the heavens, that he might fill all things.) And his gifts were that some should be apostles, some prophets, some evangelists, some pastors and teachers,

to equip the saints for the work of ministry, for building up the body of Christ, until we all attain to the unity of the faith and of the knowledge of the Son of God, to mature manhood, to the measure of the stature of the fulness of Christ.

The Gospel Reading
St. Matthew 4:12-17

At that time, when Jesus heard that John had been arrested, he withdrew into Galilee; and leaving Nazareth he went and dwelt in Capernaum by the sea, in the territory of Zebulun and Naphtali, that what was spoken by the prophet Isaiah might be fulfilled:
"The land of Zebulum and the land of Naphtali,
toward the sea, across the Jordan,
Galilee of the Gentiles —
the people who sat in darkness
have seen a great light,
and for those who sat in the region
and shadow of death light has dawned."
From that time Jesus began to preach, saying, "Repent, for the kingdom of heaven is at hand."

THE TRIODION
SUNDAY OF THE PUBLICAN

The Apostolic Reading
2 Timothy 3:10-15

Now you have observed my teaching, my conduct, my aim in life, my faith, my patience, my love, my steadfastness, my persecutions, my sufferings, what befell me at Antioch, at Ico'nium, and at Lystra, what persecutions I endured; yet from them all the Lord rescued me. Indeed all who desire to live a godly life in Christ Jesus will be persecuted, while evil men and impostors will go on from bad to worse, deceivers and deceived. But as for you, continue in what you have learned and have firmly believed, knowing from whom you learned it and how from childhood you have been acquainted with the sacred writings which are able to instruct you for salvation through faith in Christ Jesus.

The Gospel Reading
St. Luke 18:10-14

The Lord said this parable: "Two men went up into the temple to pray, one a Pharisee and the other a tax collector. The Pharisee stood and prayed thus with himself, 'God, I thank Thee that I am not like other men, extortioners, unjust, adulterers, or even like this tax collector. I fast twice a week, I give tithes of all that I get.' But the tax collector, standing far off, would not even lift up his eyes to heaven, but beat his breast, saying, 'God, be merciful to me a sinner!' I tell you, this man went down to his house justified rather than the other; for every one who exalts himself will be humbled, but he who humbles himself will be exalted."

SUNDAY OF THE PRODIGAL SON

The Apostolic Reading
I Corinthians 6:12-20

"All things are lawful for me," but not all things are helpful. "All things are lawful for me," but I will not be enslaved by anything. "Food is meant for the stomach and the stomach for food" — and God will destroy both one and the other. The body is not meant for immorality, but for the Lord, and the Lord for the body. And God raised the Lord and will also raise us up by his power. Do you not know that your bodies are members of Christ? Shall I therefore take the members of Christ and make them members of a prostitute? Never! Do you not know that he who joins himself to a prostitute becomes one body with her? For, as it is written, "The two shall become one flesh." But he who is united to the Lord becomes one spirit with him. Shun immorality. Every other sin which a man commits is outside the body; but the immoral man sins against his own body. Do you not know that your body is a temple of the Holy Spirit within you, which you have from God? You are not your own; you were bought with a price. So glorify God in your body.

The Apostolic Reading
St. Luke 15:11-32

The Lord said this parable: "There was a man who had two sons; and the younger of them said to his father, 'Father, give me the share of property that falls to me.' And he divided his living between them. Not many days later, the younger son gathered all he had and took his journey into a far country, and there he squandered his property in loose living. And when he had spent everything, a great famine arose in that country, and he began to be in want. So he went and joined himself to one of the citizens of that country, who sent him into his fields to feed swine. And he would gladly have fed on the pods that the swine ate; and no one gave him anything. But when he came to himself he said, 'How many of my father's hired servants have bread enough and to spare, but I perish here with hunger! I will arise and go to my father, and I will say to him, "Father, I have sinned against heaven and before you; I am no longer worthy to be called your son; treat me as one of your hired servants." And he arose and came to his father. But while he was yet at a distance, his father saw him and had compassion, and ran and embraced him and kissed him. And the son said to him, 'Father, I have sinned against heaven and before you; I am no longer worthy to be called your son.' But the father said to his servants, 'Bring quickly the best robe, and put it on him; and put a ring on his hand, and shoes on his feet; and bring the fatted calf and kill it, and let us eat and make merry; for this my son was dead, and is alive again; he was lost, and is found.' And they began to make merry.

"Now his elder son was in the field; and as he came and drew near to the house, he heard music and dancing. And he called one of the servants and asked what this meant. And he said to him, 'Your brother has come, and your father has killed the fatted calf, because he has received him safe and sound.' But he was angry and refused to go in. His father came out and entreated him, but he answered his father, 'Lo, these many years I have served you, and I never disobeyed your command; yet you never gave me a kid, that I might make merry with my friends. But when this son of yours came, who has devoured your living with harlots, you killed for him the fatted calf!' And he said to him, 'Son, you are always with me, and all that is mine is yours. It was fitting to make merry and be glad, for this your brother was dead, and is alive; he was lost, and is found.' "

SECOND SUNDAY BEFORE LENT
(Last day of taking meat)

The Apostolic Reading
I Corinthians 8:8-13; 9:1-2

Food will not commend us to God. We are no worse off if we do not eat, and no better off if we do. Only take care lest this liberty of yours somehow become a stumbling block to the weak. For if any one sees you, a man of knowledge, at table in an idol's temple, might he not be encouraged, if his conscience is weak, to eat food offered to idols? And so by your knowledge this weak man is destroyed, the brother for whom Christ died. Thus, sinning against your brethren and wounding their conscience when it is weak, you sin against Christ. Therefore, if food is a cause of my brother's falling, I will never eat meat, lest I cause my brother to fall.

Am I not free? Am I not an apostle? Have I not seen Jesus our Lord? Are not you my workmanship in the Lord? If to others I am not an apostle, at least I am to you; for you are the seal of my apostleship in the Lord.

The Gospel Reading
St. Matthew 25:31-46

The Lord said: "When the Son of man comes in his glory, and all the angels with him, then he will sit on his glorious throne. Before him will be gathered all the nations, and he will separate them one from another as a shepherd separates the sheep from the goats, and he will place the sheep at his right hand, but the goats at the left. Then the King will say to those at his right hand, 'Come, O blessed of My Father, inherit the king-

dom prepared for you from the foundation of the world; for I was hungry and you gave me food, I was thirsty and you gave me drink, I was a stranger and you welcomed me, I was naked and you clothed me, I was sick and you visited me, I was in prison and you came to me.' Then the righteous will answer him, 'Lord, when did we see Thee hungry and feed Thee, or thirsty and give Thee drink? And when did we see Thee a stranger and welcome Thee, or naked and clothe Thee? And when did we see Thee sick or in prison and visit Thee?' And the King will answer them, 'Truly, I say to you, as you did it to one of the least of these my brethren, you did it to me.' Then he will say to those at his left hand, 'Depart from me, you cursed, into the eternal fire prepared for the devil and his angels; for I was hungry and you gave me no food, I was thirsty and you gave me no drink, I was a stranger and you did not welcome me, naked and you did not clothe me, sick and in prison and you did not visit me.' Then they also will answer, 'Lord, when did we see Thee hungry or thirsty or a stranger or naked or sick or in prison, and did not minister to Thee?' Then he will answer them, 'Truly, I say to you, as you did it not to one of the least of these, you did it not to me.' And they will go away into eternal punishment, but the righteous into eternal life."

LAST SUNDAY BEFORE LENT
(Last day of taking dairy products)
The Apostolic Reading
Romans 13:11-14; 14:1-4

Besides this you know what hour it is, how it is full time now for you to wake from sleep. For salvation is nearer to us now than when we first believed; the night is far gone, the day is at hand. Let us then cast off the works of darkness and put on the armor of light; let us conduct ourselves becomingly as in the day, not in reveling and drunkenness, not in debauchery and licentiousness, not in quarreling and jealousy. But put on the Lord Jesus Christ, and make no provision for the flesh, to gratify its desires.

As for the man who is weak in faith, welcome him, but not for disputes over opinions. One believes he may eat anything, while the weak man eats only vegetables. Let not him who eats despise him who abstains, and let not him who abstains pass judgment on him who eats; for God has welcomed him. Who are you to pass judgment on the servant of another? It is before his own master that he stands or falls. And he will be upheld, for the Master is able to make him stand.

The Gospel Reading
St. Matthew 6:14-21

The Lord said: "If you forgive men their trespasses, your heavenly Father also will forgive you; but if you do not forgive men their trespasses, neither will your Father forgive your trespasses.

"And when you fast, do not look dismal, like the hypocrites, for they disfigure their faces that their fasting may be seen by men. Truly, I say to you, they have their reward. But when you fast, anoint your head and wash your face, that your fasting may not be seen by men but by your Father who is in secret; and your Father who sees in secret will reward you.

"Do not lay up for yourselves treasures on earth, where moth and rust consume and where thieves break in and steal, but lay up for yourselves treasures in heaven, where neither moth nor rust consumes and where thieves do not break in and steal. For where your treasure is, there will your heart be also.

THE GREAT LENT
FIRST SUNDAY
(Sunday of Orthodoxy)

The Apostolic Reading
Hebrews 11:24-26; 32-40; 12:1-2

And what more shall I say? For time would fail me to tell of Gideon, Barak, Samson, Jephthah, of David and Samuel and the prophets — who through faith conquered kingdoms, enforced justice, received promises, stopped the mouths of lions, quenched raging fire, escaped the edge of the sword, won strength out of weakness, became mighty in war, put foreign armies to flight. Women received their dead by resurrection. Some were tortured, refusing to accept release, that they might rise again to a better life. Others suffered mocking and scourging, and even chains and imprisonment. They were stoned, they were sawn in two, they were killed with the sword; they went about in skins of sheep and goats, destitute, afflicted, ill-treated — of whom the world was not worthy — wandering over deserts and mountains, and in dens and caves of the earth.

And all these, though well attested by their faith, did not receive what was promised, since God had foreseen something better for us, that apart from us they should not be made perfect.

By faith Moses, when he was grown up, refused to be called the son of Pharaoh's daughter, choosing rather to share ill-treatment with the people of God than to enjoy the fleeting pleasures of sin. He considered abuse suffered for the Christ greater wealth than the treasures of Egypt, for he looked to the reward.

Therefore, since we are surrounded by so great a cloud of witnesses, let us also lay aside every weight, and sin which clings so closely, and let us run with perseverance the race that is set before us, looking to Jesus the pioneer and perfecter of our faith, who for the joy that was set before him endured the cross, despising the shame, and is seated at the right hand of the throne of God.

The Gospel Reading
St. John 1:43-52

At that time, Jesus decided to go to Galilee. And he found Philip and said to him, "Follow me." Now Philip was from Bethsaida, the city of Andrew and Peter. Philip found Nathanael, and said to him, "We have found him of whom Moses in the law and also the prophets wrote, Jesus of Nazareth, the son of Joseph." Nathanael said to him, "Can anything good come out of Nazareth?" Philip said to him, "Come and see." Jesus saw Nathanael coming to him, and said of him, "Behold, an Israelite indeed, in whom is no guile!" Nathanael said to him, "How do you know me?" Jesus answered him, "Before Philip called you, when you were under the fig tree, I saw you." Nathanael answered him, "Rabbi, you are the Son of God! You are the King of Israel!" Jesus answered him, "Because I said to you, I saw you under the fig tree, do you believe? You shall see greater things than these." And he said to him, "Truly, truly, I say to you, you will see heaven opened, and the angels of God ascending and descending upon the Son of man."

SECOND SUNDAY

The Apostolic Reading
Hebrews 1:10-14; 2:1-3

"Thou, Lord, didst found the earth in the beginning, and the heavens are the work of thy hands; they will perish, but Thou remainest; they will all grow old like a garment, like a mantle Thou wilt roll them up, and they will be changed. But Thou art the same, and thy years will never end." But to what angel has he ever said, "Sit at my right hand, till I make thy enemies a stool for thy feet"? Are they not all ministering spirits sent forth to serve, for the sake of those who are to obtain salvation?

Therefore we must pay the closer attention to what we have heard, lest we drift away from it. For if the message declared by angels was valid and every transgression or disobedience received a just retribution, how shall we escape if we neglect such a great salvation?

The Gospel Reading
St. Mark 2:1-12

At that time, Jesus entered Capernaum and it was reported that he was at home. And many were gathered together, so that there was no longer room for them, not even about the door; and he was preaching the word to them. And they came, bringing to him a paralytic carried by four men. And when they could not get near him because of the crowd, they removed the roof above him; and when they had made an opening, they let down the pallet on which the paralytic lay. And when Jesus saw their faith, he said to the paralytic, "My son, your sins are forgiven." Now some of the scribes were sitting there, questioning in their hearts, "Why does this man speak thus? It is blasphemy! Who can forgive sins but God alone?" And immediately Jesus, perceiving in his spirit that they thus questioned within themselves, said to them, "Why do you question thus in your hearts? Which is easier, to say to the paralytic, 'Your sins are forgiven,' or to say, 'Rise, take up your pallet and walk'? But that you may know that the Son of man has authority on earth to forgive sins" — he said to the paralytic — "I say to you, rise, take up your pallet and go home." And he rose, and immediately took up the pallet and went out before them all; so that they were all amazed and glorified God, saying. "We never saw anything like this!"

THIRD SUNDAY

The Apostolic Reading
Hebrews 4:14-15; 5:1-6

Since then we have a great high priest who has passed through the heavens, Jesus, the Son of God, let us hold fast our confession. For we have not a high priest who is unable to sympathize with our weaknesses, but one who in every respect has been tempted as we are, yet without sin.

For every high priest chosen from among men is appointed to act on behalf of men in relation to God, to offer gifts and sacrifices for sins. He can deal gently with the ignorant and wayward, since he himself is beset with weakness. Because of this he is bound to offer sacrifice for his own sins as well as for those of the people. And one does not take the honor upon himself, but he is called by God, just as Aaron was.

So also Christ did not exalt himself to be made a high priest, but was appointed by him who said to him,

"Thou art my Son,
today I have begotten Thee";
as he says also in another place,
"Thou art a priest for ever,
after the order of Melchiz'edek."

The Gospel Reading
St. Mark 8:34-38, 9:1

The Lord said: "If anyone wishes to come after me, let him deny himself and take up his cross and follow me. For whoever would save his life will lose it; and whoever loses his life for my sake and the gospel's will save it. For what does it profit a man, to gain the whole world and forfeit his life? For what can a man give in return for his life? For whoever is ashamed of me and of my words in this adulterous and sinful generation, of him will the Son of man also be ashamed, when he comes in the glory of his Father with the holy angels." And he said to them, "Truly, I say to you, there are some standing here who will not taste death before they see the kingdom of God come with power."

FOURTH SUNDAY

The Apostolic Reading
Hebrews 6:13-20

For when God made a promise to Abraham, since he had no one greater by whom to swear, he swore by himself, saying, "Surely I will bless you and multiply you." And thus Abraham, having patiently endured, obtained the promise. Men indeed swear by a greater than themselves, and in all their disputes an oath is final for confirmation. So when God desired to show more convincingly to the heirs of the promise the unchangeable character of his purpose, he interposed with an oath, so that through two unchangeable things, in which it is impossible that God should prove false, we who have field for refuge might have strong encouragement to seize the hope set before us. We have this as a sure and steadfast anchor of the soul, a hope that enters into the inner shrine behind the curtain, where Jesus has gone as a forerunner on our behalf, having become a high priest for ever after the order of Melchiz'edek.

The Gospel Reading
St. Mark 9:17-31

At that time, a man came to Jesus kneeling and saying: "Teacher, I brought my son to you, for he has a dumb spirit; and wherever it seizes him, it dashes him down; and he foams and grinds his teeth and becomes rigid; and I asked your disciples to cast it out, and they were not able." And he answered them, "O faithless generation, how long am I to be with you? How long am I to bear with you? Bring him to me." And they brought the boy to him; and when the spirit saw him, immediately it convulsed the boy, and he fell on the ground and rolled about, foaming at the mouth. And Jesus asked his father, "How long has he had this?" And he said, "From childhood. And it has often cast him into the fire and into the water, to destroy him; but if you can do anything, have pity on us and help us." And Jesus said to him, "If you can! All things are possible to him who believes." Immediately the father of the child cried out and said, "I believe; help my unbelief!" And when Jesus saw that a crowd came running together, he rebuked the unclean spirit, saying to it, "You dumb and deaf spirit, I command you, come out of him, and never enter him again." And after crying out and convulsing him terribly, it came out, and the boy was like a corpse; so that most of them said, "He is dead." But Jesus took him by the hand and lifted him up, and he arose. And when he had entered the house, his disciples asked him privately, "Why could we not cast it out?" And he said to them, "This kind cannot be driven out by anything but prayer and fasting."

They went on from there and passed through Galilee. And he would not have any one know it; for he was teaching his disciples, saying to them, "The Son of man will be delivered into the hands of men, and they will kill him; and when he is killed, after three days he will rise."

FIFTH SUNDAY
The Apostolic Reading
Hebrews 9:11-14

But when Christ appeared as a high priest of the

good things that have come, then through the greater and more perfect tent (not made with hands, that is, not of this creation) he entered once for all into the Holy Place, taking not the blood of goats and calves but his own blood, thus securing an eternal redemption. For if the sprinkling of defiled persons with the blood of goats and bulls and with the ashes of a heifer sanctified for the purification of the flesh, how much more shall the blood of Christ, who through the eternal Spirit offered himself without blemish to God, purify your conscience from dead works to serve the living God.

The Gospel Reading
St. Mark 10:32-45

At that time, Jesus taking the twelve again, he began to tell them what was to happen to him, saying, "Behold, we are going up to Jerusalem; and the Son of man will be delivered to the chief priests and the scribes, and they will condemn him to death, and deliver him to the Gentiles; and they will mock him, and spit upon him, and scourge him, and kill him; and after three days he will rise."

And James and John, the sons of Zebedee, came forward to him, and said to him, "Teacher, we want you to do for us whatever we ask of you." And he said to them, "What do you want me to do for you?" And they said to him, "Grant us to sit, one at your right hand and one at your left, in your glory." But Jesus said to them, "You do not know what you are asking. Are you able to drink the cup that I drink, or to be baptized with the baptism with which I am baptized?" And they said to him, "We are able." And Jesus said to them, "The cup that I drink you will drink; and with the baptism with which I am baptized, you will be baptized; but to sit at my right hand or at my left is not mine to grant, but it is for those for whom it has been prepared." And when the ten heard it, they began to be indignant at James and John. And Jesus called them to him and said to them, "You know that those who are supposed to rule over the Gentiles lord it over them, and their great men exercise authority over them. But it shall not be so among you; but whoever would be great among you must be your servant, and whoever would be first among you must be slave of all. For the Son of man also came not to be served but to serve, and to give his life as a ransom for many."

PALM SUNDAY

The Apostolic Reading
Philippians 4:4-9

Brethren, rejoice in the Lord always; again I will say, Rejoice. Let all men know your forbearance. The Lord is at hand. Have no anxiety about anything, but in everything by prayer and supplication with thanksgiving let your requests be made known to God. And the peace of God, which passes all understanding, will keep your hearts and your minds in Christ Jesus.

Finally, brethren, whatever is true, whatever is honorable, whatever is just, whatever is pure, whatever is lovely, whatever is gracious, if there is any excellence, if there is anything worthy of praise, think about these things. What you have learned and received and heard and seen in me; and the God of peace will be with you.

The Gospel Reading
St. John 12:1-18

Six days before the Passover, Jesus came to Bethany,

where Lazarus was, whom Jesus had raised from the dead. There they made him a supper; Martha served, and Lazarus was one of those at table with him. Mary took a pound of costly ointment of pure nard and anointed the feet of Jesus and wiped his feet with her hair; and the house was filled with the fragrance of the ointment. But Judas Iscariot, one of his disciples (he who was to betray him), said "Why was this ointment not sold for three hundred denarii and given to the poor?" This he said, not that he cared for the poor but because he was a thief, and as he had the money box he used to take what was put into it. Jesus said, "Let her alone, let her keep it for the day of my burial. The poor you always have with you, but you do not always have me."

When the great crowd of the Jews learned that he was there, they came, not only on account of Jesus but also to see Lazarus, whom he had raised from the dead. So the chief priests planned to put Lazarus also to death, because on account of him many of the Jews were going away and believing in Jesus.

The next day a great crowd who had come to the feast heard that Jesus was coming to Jerusalem. So they took branches of palm trees and went out to meet him, crying, "Hosanna! Blessed is he who comes in the name of the Lord, even the King of Israel!" And Jesus found a young ass and sat upon it; as it is written,

"Fear not, daughter of Zion;
behold, your king is coming,
sitting on an ass's colt!"

His disciples did not understand this at first; but when Jesus was glorified, then they remembered that this had been written of him and had been done to him. The crowd that had been with him when he called

Lazarus out of the tomb and raised him from the dead bore witness. The reason why the crowd went to meet him was that they heard he had done this sign.

HOLY FRIDAY

The Apostolic Reading
I Corinthians 5:6-8

Do you not know that a little leaven leavens the whole lump? Cleanse out the old leaven that you may be a new lump, as you really are unleavened. For Christ, our paschal lamb, has been sacrified. Let us, therefore, celebrate the festival, not with the old leaven, the leaven of malice and evil, but with the unleavened bread of sincerity and truth.

Galatians 3:13-14

Christ redeemed us from the curse of the law, having become a curse for us — for it is written, "Cursed be every one who hangs on a tree" — that in Christ Jesus the blessing of Abraham might come upon the Gentiles, that we might receive the promise of the Spirit through faith.

The Gospel Reading
St. Matthew 27:62-66

The next day, that is, after the day of Preparation, the chief priests and the Pharisees gathered before Pilate and said, "Sir, we remember how that impostor said, while he was still alive, 'After three days I will rise again.' Therefore order the sepulchre to be made secure until the third day, lest his disciples go and steal him away, and tell the people, 'He has risen from the dead, and the last fraud will be worse than the first. Pilate said to them, "You have a guard of soldiers; go, make it secure as you can." So they went and made the sepulchre secure by sealing the stone and setting a guard.

HOLY SATURDAY
The Apostolic Reading
Romans 6:3-11

Brethren, do you not know that all of us who have been baptized into Christ Jesus were baptized into his death? We were buried therefore with him by baptism into death, so that as Christ was raised from the dead by the glory of the Father, we too might walk in newness of life.

For if we have been united with him in a death like his, we shall certainly be united with him in a resurrection like his. We know that our old self was crucified with him so that the sinful body might be destroyed, and we might no longer be enslaved to sin. For he who has died is freed from sin. But if we have died with Christ, we believe that we shall also live with him. For we know that Christ being raised from the dead will never die again; death no longer has dominion over him. The death he died he died to sin, once for all, but the life he lives he lives to God. So you also must consider yourselves dead to sin and alive to God in Christ Jesus.

The Gospel Reading
St. Matthew 28:1-20

After the sabbath, toward the dawn of the first day of the week, Mary Mag'dalene and the other Mary went to see the sepulchre. And behold, there was a great earthquake; for an angel of the Lord descended from heaven and came and rolled back the stone, and sat upon it. His appearance was like lightning, and his raiment white as snow. And for fear of him the guards trembled and became like dead men. But the angel said to the women, "Do not be afraid; for I know that you seek Jesus who was crucified. He is not here; for he has risen, as he said. Come, see the place where he lay. Then go quickly and tell his disciples that he has risen from the dead, and behold, he is going before you to Galilee; there you will see him. Lo, I have told you." So they departed quickly from the tomb with fear and great joy, and ran to tell his disciples. And behold, Jesus met them and said, "Hail!" And they came up and took hold of his feet and worshiped him. Then Jesus said to them, "Do not be afraid; go and tell my brethren to go to Galilee, and there they will see me."

While they were going, behold, some of the guard went into the city and told the chief priests all that had taken place. And when they had assembled with the elders and taken counsel, they gave a sum of money to the soldiers and said, "Tell people, 'His disciples came by night and stole him away while we were asleep.' And if this comes to the governor's ears, we will satisfy him and keep you out of trouble." So they took the money and did as they were directed; and his story has been spread among the Jews to this day.

Now the eleven disciples went to Galilee, to the mountain to which Jesus had directed them. And when they saw him they worshiped him; but some doubted. And Jesus came and said to them, "All authority in heaven and on earth has been given to me. Go therefore and make disciples of all nations, baptizing them in the name of the Father and of the Son and of the Holy Spirit, teaching them to observe all that I have commanded you; and lo, I am with you always, to the close of the age."